Volume 3

Living in Geulah

How to Survive & Thrive During the Transformation of the World from Chaos to Divine Revelation

Artnotes By Rae Shagalov

from the Global Geula Summit Hosted By Shifra Chana Hendrie

Printed in the United States of America
First Printing 2020
ISBN: 978-1-937472-11-5

www.HOLYSPARKS.COM
©2020 Rae Shagalov

Gimmel Tammuz 5780
Los Angeles

Contact Rae Shagalov
E-mail: info • holysparks.com

- For wholesale discounts and bulk discounts for groups and teachers
- To arrange a creative workshop or author event with Rae Shagalov
- For custom calligraphy or Artnotes from classes, live or recorded
- To dedicate a volume in the Joyfully Jewish series
  in memory or honor of someone special
- **To commission a book like this created for you
  without you having to write a word!**

Holy Sparks Press
WWW.HOLYSPARKS.COM

Please do not color on Shabbat or Jewish holy days,
as writing and coloring are prohibited by Jewish Law on those days.

בס"ד

This is a gift for:

From:

May you be blessed
with success
and only good things

❧PRAISE FOR RAE SHAGALOV'S JOYFULLY JEWISH ARTNOTES ❧

"TAKE A CREATIVE JOURNEY INTO YOUR JEWISH SOUL! Rae's delightful illustrations and inspiring words take you step by step into pure connection, relaxation and visualized tranquility."   *-B. B. Romm-*

"FULL OF COOL THINGS TO COLOR! It's not only full of cool things to color.....each page is a whole 'lesson' for a JOYFUL JEWISH LIFE!!! I can't wait to give them to friends, family, and of course, to get coloring!!!!"   *-Malka F.-*

"I FEEL CALMER AND HAPPIER! Rae's Artnotes make me feel calmer and help me correct my negative thoughts. I love how her art brings me into my center and helps me to remember what is important and what is not – and that my priority needs to be to serve Hashem b'simcha, with joy, no matter what!" *-Shoshanna P.-*

"BEAUTIFUL AND DEEP! I was inspired by the beautiful art and deep, important, and Chassidic topics Rae chose to write about, clearly written with love and a deep caring for a fellow Jew." *– Elisheva K., Chabad House, Washington Heights, NYC-*

"STUDY AND UNDERSTAND TORAH! Although I'm not Jewish, Rae's artwork and quotes have deepened my desire to study and understand Torah and the G-d of Abraham, Isaac, and Jacob. Rae's joyful attitude toward G-d is compelling and inviting."   *-Tracy T, Kansas-*

"SPIRITUALLY UPLIFTING! This is the most spiritually uplifting experience a family or individual can do! Opportunity to be creative and also touch that still small voice we often miss in this noisy world!"   *-W.S.-*

"THE CALLIGRAPHY IS MAGNIFICENT! What a beautiful book. The writings are so very inspirational and the calligraphy is magnificent."   *-Phaedra-*

LITTLE BOOSTS OF LIGHT! "I surround myself with Rae's art in my home office. I love that whenever I get overwhelmed or discouraged, I can just look up and the Holy Sparks Artnotes are like little boosts of light that help me turn my dark thoughts into positive action."

-Esther G., Producer of "Lights and Miracle Days"-

"BEAUTIFUL, UPLIFTING WISDOM! Such beautiful, uplifting wisdom in such a short amount of words! I keep buying more of these to give out to my friends."

-A.N.-

❧ CONTENTS ❧

❧ INDEX OF TEACHERS ❧

❧ HOW TO USE THIS BOOK ❧

SURROUND YOURSELF WITH INSPIRATION, ART & FRIENDS

Invite your family and friends to join you in the fun. Feel free to take this book apart and share the pages or have some extra copies of the book on hand to share or give as gifts. Hang up the Artnotes that inspire you the most, just as they are, or colored in by you, your family, and your friends. Surround yourself with this love and inspiration to keep you moving forward and higher in your life and work.

This book is not intended to be read from beginning to end in one sitting. The pages do not need to be read in order. You can skip around to what attracts you the most, read from beginning to end, or open to a random page. You can simply enjoy the calligraphy Artnotes and let the deep Jewish wisdom seep into your soul and inspire you, or you can interact with the wisdom playfully by coloring in the images, writing and doodling on the journal pages, and engaging in the Soul Adventures.

ENJOY YOUR SOUL ADVENTURES

I've also included Soul Adventures to help you integrate the profound Jewish wisdom you'll be learning in this book. What is a Soul Adventure? A Soul Adventure is a journey above time and space to explore the vast, fascinating chambers of your own soul and the G-dly hints, echoes, whispers, and holy sparks that are hidden in your innermost self. Soul Adventures are creative exercises that help you look deeply at your life and make significant, transformative changes to improve it.

CREATE A JOURNAL IN THE BOOK

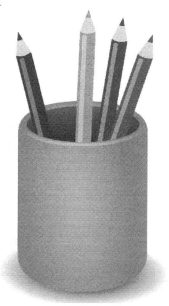

There are journal pages in the book for you to record any insights and challenges that arise when you read through the Artnotes. You can also use these journal pages to doodle or write poetry, imagine or envision what you hope your life can be, or to use creatively in any way you choose. Explore your inner world through the prompts provided in each Soul Adventure. Sketch and twirl your pen in between writing your thoughts or if you feel stuck and unable to write. These doodles will relax and focus you and may provide a wealth of understanding of the subconscious and sublime whispers of your G-dly soul.

COLOR IT IN!

Coloring is a very relaxing, peaceful, meditative activity. As you color in the pages, contemplate the Artnotes thoughts on them and try to internalize them. If you're doing this as a family activity, discuss the ideas while you color them in together. Afterwards, hang up these beautiful family treasures around your home to set a Joyfully Jewish tone.

Coloring can help you relax into a peaceful and contemplative mood, so turn off the phone, computer and any other stressful distractions. For best results, use colored pencils. Place a piece of cardboard or a few sheets of paper underneath the page if you are using pens so the ink won't bleed through.

Gather your colored pencils or pens. Flip through the book and choose a page that sparks your interest. Intuitively choose your colors and don't fret if you make a "mistake" or color outside the lines. Just relax and continue, letting your mind wander and enjoy the colors. Being in this relaxed state will improve your life and outlook, but you can also use it to go higher into holiness. How do you do this?

You could listen to a Torah class while coloring, or you could meditate on the greatness of G-d. When you are in this relaxed state, it is a very good time to think about and speak to G-d. It's a wonderful place to be in to think about your life, your family and friends and how you can improve yourself and your relationships.

It's a lovely interlude for creatively thinking about a new mitzvah you would like to do, or imagining how you could do a mitzvah more beautifully than before. It's a special time to dream about what the world will be like when Moshiach comes, G-d willing, very, very soon to usher in the great era of peace that we all wait and wish for. When you do this, you elevate the act of coloring by serving G-d with it.

❧ INTRODUCTION ❧

The world is changing so fast. None of us expected that the world would look anything like this! And it keeps changing dramatically every day.

But what if you knew that there is a vast cosmic purpose driving these changes? What if you understood that the breakdown of the old is ushering in a massive new divine potential for the whole world? What if you had the knowledge and wisdom to safely and peacefully navigate the waves of change in the world and in your own life?

Shifra Chana Hendrie's "Global Geula Summit" was an extraordinary series of conversations with global Jewish leaders, teachers, and healers sharing the deepest secrets of creation and our special role in this momentous time in Jewish and human history. It's called Geulah – that wonderful time of peace and plenty we all long for when the whole world will be filled with the knowledge of G-d.

Volume 3 of the Joyfully Jewish series, "Living Geulah" records the highlights of these fascinating interviews between Shifra Chana and these 24 life-changing teachers.*

A new reality is emerging, the rectification of the world and all of human history. As the cosmic awakening moves forward, there are increasing opportunities for us to make a really significant impact on how things unfold, as we partner with G-d to bring in this new, harmonious world.

In this collection of Artnotes, you will find much wisdom and many actionable tips and meditations to help you stay calm in these chaotic times, and thrive in the threshold of Geulah. And if you enjoy the relaxing art of coloring, the illustrations are perfect for you.

So relax and enjoy the journey as you immerse in the wisdom of this transformational time of living in Geulah.

---

*You can purchase recordings of the Global Geulah Summit, find out more about Shifra Chana, and join her Gate of Unity School at: www.gateofunity.com

בס"ד

A new world
is emerging.

We shouldn't be
scared, we should
just be prepared
for all the good
that's coming.

ALANA YAKOVLEV

Holy Sparks
WWW.HOLYSPARKS.COM
©2020 Rae Shagalov

9

With Deep Appreciation & Gratitude to Shifra Chana Hendrie for a truly life-changing Geula Summit, & to all of the extraordinary speakers who inspired these Artnotes.

Sign up for your FREE bonus at:
HOLYSPARKS.COM
(Feel free to share this link with your friends!)

LET'S CONNECT!
Facebook.com/soultips
Pinterest.com/holysparks
Twitter.com/holysparks
Youtube.com/holysparksbooks
Instagram.com/holysparks

I would love to hear your insights and questions and see your colorful creations, so let's connect! Feel free to email me with questions, suggestions & pictures of your coloring:
info • holysparks.com

~ Rae's Artist's Statement ~

"Any mistakes contained herein are my own. Although my Artnotes artistically capture some of the deep insights of these masters of Torah, my notes cannot convey the warmth, caring, humor, incredible stories, and intellectual challenge you will experience when you hear them, in person or on recordings."

Sign up to receive FREE art, coloring pages, & Rae Shagalov's Soul Tips newsletter with calligraphy Artnotes & important spiritual tips for our chaotic times.
WWW.HOLYSPARKS.COM

These Hebrew letters appear at the top of each Artnotes page:

בס״ד

This is an abbreviation for the Aramaic phrase "B'Sayata Di'Shmaya,"
which means, "With the Help of Heaven."

OR

בי״ה

This is an abbreviation for Baruch Hashem (Blessed is the Name of G-d
or B'ezrat Hashem (With the help of G-d)

Putting these letters at the top of every page reminds us that everything
comes from G-d and that we need His help in everything we do.

Throughout the text, the variant spellings *geula* and *geulah* are used interchangeably.

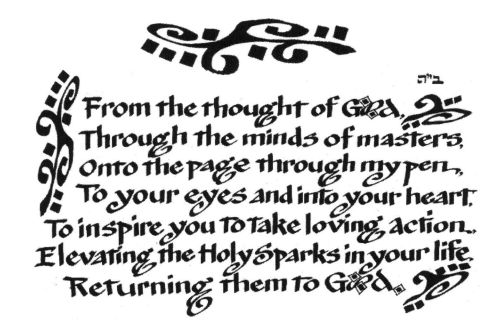

From the thought of G-d,
Through the minds of masters,
Onto the page through my pen,
To your eyes and into your heart,
To inspire you to take loving action,
Elevating the Holy Sparks in your life,
Returning them to G-d.

13

There is light within the darkness, and darkness within the light. It's a journey, part of a process.

CONNECT WITH A PERSON WHERE THEY ARE ~ NOT WHERE YOU ARE.

YOU HAVE AN IMPORTANT ROLE IN THIS COSMIC JOURNEY.

WE NEED YOU!

WHEN YOU FULFILL YOUR PURPOSE, YOU HELP ALL OF US.

WE ARE AT THE END OF THE PROCESS.

We are agents of light!

ALL OF OUR GOOD DEEDS AND SUFFERING ARE ABOUT TO TRANSFORM THE WORLD INTO THE ULTIMATE GARDEN OF G-D.

The darkness is only to reveal a higher light.

G‑d provides the garden. We are the gardeners, weeding the flowers of our soul.

Your part

IS TO USE YOUR SKILLS, YOUR TALENTS, YOUR CIRCUMSTANCES, YOUR LIMITATIONS AND ALL OF YOUR RESOURCES AND EMOTIONS, LIGHT AND DARKNESS, TO REVEAL WHAT IS HOLY AND WEED OUT WHAT IS NOT.

Your mission is essential to all of us.

MY IDENTITY IS NOT DEFINED BY THE INJUSTICES THAT HAVE BEEN DONE TO ME.

TECHNOLOGY IS MEANT TO HELP US TRANSFORM THIS WORLD TO HIGHER CONSCIOUSNESS.

"CONVERSATIONS FROM THE EDGE OF HUMAN POTENTIAL"

Global Geula Summit

"FROM SURVIVAL TO A MISSION-DRIVEN LIFE"

RABBI SIMON JACOBSON
SHIFRA CHANA HENDRIE

Holy Sparks

בס"ד

Where are you?

WE ARE NOT HERE JUST TO BATTLE DARKNESS. WE ARE HERE TO BRING LIGHT.

There is more light than darkness!

THERE IS A REALITY THAT TRANSCENDS PAIN AND JOY, DARK AND LIGHT.

Listen deeply for the answer.

Begin with Compassion

"I'M WITH YOU. I LOVE YOU. WE WILL GET THROUGH THIS."

Connect to the Source.

PREPARE FOR THE DARK TIMES. BY STRENGTHENING YOUR CONNECTION TO G-D IN THE TIMES OF LIGHT. THIS GIVES US THE COURAGE TO NAVIGATE THROUGH THE DARKNESS.

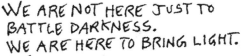

Your darkness is only to bring a deeper light.

It is only through darkness that you can reach levels of light that are beyond light itself.

How can you transform your challenges into opportunities?

THE JEWISH PEOPLE HAVE BUILT UP RESILIENCE OVER 4,000 YEARS

"CONVERSATIONS FROM THE EDGE OF HUMAN POTENTIAL"

Global Geula Summit
"FROM SURVIVAL TO A MISSION-DRIVEN LIFE"

RABBI SIMON JACOBSON
SHIFRA CHANA HENDRIE

Holy Sparks

WWW.HOLYSPARKS.COM
©2020 Rae Shagalov
15

Create your mission statement:

SOUL ADVENTURE #1

Look for spiritual opportunities wherever you go.

Create your mission statement:

Your mission statement should be:

◆ Unique
◆ Specific
◆ Short
◆ Serves a purpose

① List every thing you do in a day.

② Look at this map of your day. Connect each activity to your mission. What can you add or subtract in your day to focus more on your mission?

③ Look for patterns that point to your mission. Strengthen those connections.

What is my role? Where is the light in the darkness?

Focus on your mission.

Align all of your actions with your mission.

בּ"ה

Address issues at the root, not just the symptom.

Reactive or Proactive

Focusing on your mission allows you to take control of your reaction.

"What is this calling out of me to bring me to higher consciousness?"

Find a mentor to help you.

WHEN SOMETHING NEGATIVE HAPPENS, ASK:

How does this fit into my mission?

Become one with your Source

Your soul should control the activities of your body.

THE TRUTH IS EMBEDDED IN ALL OF EXISTENCE.

"CONVERSATIONS FROM THE EDGE OF HUMAN POTENTIAL"

RABBI SIMON JACOBSON
SHIFRA CHANA HENDRIE

Global Geula Summit

"FROM SURVIVAL TO A MISSION-DRIVEN LIFE"

Holy Sparks

WWW.HOLYSPARKS.COM
©2020 Rae Shagalov

SOUL ADVENTURE #2

Look for the miracles in your life
and record them here.

בס"ד

בס"ד

Everything G-d created in this world He created to express His glory. EVERYTHING IN THIS WORLD HAS A HIGHER PURPOSE TO IT.

IN A COMPLEX WORLD...

Be simple.

◆ Authentic
◆ Sincere

Geulah is built into this world.

The Tzaddik

MIRRORS TO US OUR HIGHEST POTENTIAL.

◆ Create TRUE CONNECTION Community.

COMMUNITY WILL FOSTER THE GEULAH.

◆ Make time for your true inner self.

CULTIVATE 'DAAT,' THE MERGING OF MIND AND EMOTION. STUDY CHASSIDUS BEFORE YOU PRAY, IN THE MORNING.

3 Levels of Miracles

① ABOVE NATURE
② WITHIN NATURE BUT WE ONLY SEE IT IN RETROSPECT
③ THE HIGHEST LEVEL OF MIRACLES IS IN NATURE BUT ONLY G-D SEES IT. MOSHIACH WILL REVEAL TO US THE INFINITE POTENTIAL WITHIN CREATION.

Recognize the miraculous in your every day Life.

Open your eyes!

OPEN YOUR EYES AND SEE G-D'S GOODNESS AND MIRACLES EVERYWHERE!

"HEAVEN MEETS EARTH: SCIENCE, SPIRITUALITY & MIRACLES"   RABBI AMICHAI COHEN
SHIFRA CHANA HENDRIE

"CONVERSATIONS FROM THE EDGE OF HUMAN POTENTIAL"

Global Geula Summit

Holy Sparks

WWW.HOLYSPARKS.COM
©2020 Rae Shagalov

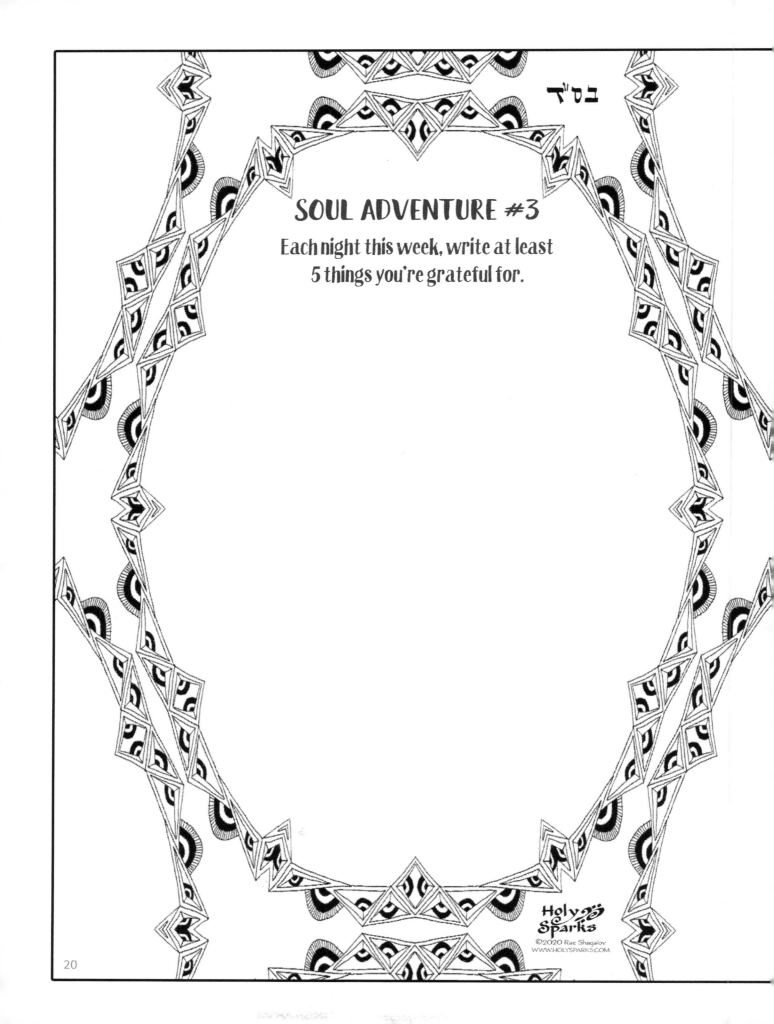

בס"ד

SOUL ADVENTURE #3

Each night this week, write at least
5 things you're grateful for.

CULTIVATE YOUR AWARENESS OF G-D.

Focus on the Good

in your life.

WRITE 5 THINGS YOU'RE GRATEFUL FOR IN YOUR DAY, EVERY NIGHT.

The things that happen are G-d dialoguing with us.

Don't break. Connect and integrate.

THE ALEF IS THE FIRST LETTER OF THE HEBREW ALPHABET AND HOLDS WITHIN IT THE HOLY ENERGY OF ALL SUBSEQUENT LETTERS. G-D CREATED THE WORLD THROUGH THE HOLY LETTERS.

In the merit of the righteous women we will be redeemed...

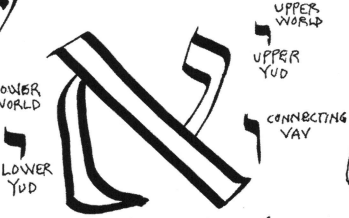

LOWER WORLD

LOWER YUD

UPPER WORLD

UPPER YUD

CONNECTING VAV

Alef Meditation

BREATHE AND LET GO OF ALL WORRY AND ANXIETY. VISUALIZE THE ALEF SHINING FORTH ITS RADIANT ENERGY AND VITALITY. SEE THE ALEF GROWING LARGER, FILLING THE SPACE. CONNECT TO THE SOURCE ROOT OF THE UPPER ALEF BEAMING ITS INTENSE RADIANT ENERGY PERMEATING YOU AS IT FLOWS AND BINDS TO THE CONNECTING VAV, DRAWING THE VITALITY DEEPER INTO YOUR MIND AND EXISTENCE, VITALIZING THE LOWER YUD. FEEL IT ENERGIZING YOU, YOUR BODY, AND THE WORLD.

"HEAVEN MEETS EARTH: SCIENCE, SPIRITUALITY & MIRACLES"

RABBI AMICHAI COHEN
SHIFRA CHANA HENDRIE

"CONVERSATIONS FROM THE EDGE OF HUMAN POTENTIAL"
Global Geula Summit

Holy Sparks

SOUL ADVENTURE #4

How can you push beyond your limits?
What can you transform this week?
How can you re-create yourself today?

It's time to want change instead of resisting change.

IT'S GOOD TO WANT TO FIT IN AND FEEL FAMILIAR AND COMFORTABLE, BUT IT'S ALSO GOOD TO PUT YOURSELF IN AWKWARD, UNCOMFORTABLE SITUATIONS TO STRETCH YOURSELF BEYOND YOUR LIMITATIONS. THIS IS HOW YOU LEARN WHO YOU ARE AND WHO YOU CAN BE, WHEN YOU TEST YOUR BOUNDARIES, AND PUSH BEYOND YOURSELF.

Infinite Elevations

How can I push my own limits?

HOW CAN YOU BE TRANSFORMED EVERY WEEK?

It's time to Be excited about the wonder and delight of uncertainty.

Continuous recreation of ourselves, our world, and our reality is like being in a non-stop surprise party.

Embrace the adventure of Geula so that it can flow through you.

Enjoy your process ✦ progress ✦ journey.

RABBI ASHER CRISPE
SHIFRA CHANA HENDRIE

"THE MIRACULOUS FUTURE EMERGING TODAY"
Global Geula Summit
"CONVERSATIONS FROM THE EDGE OF HUMAN POTENTIAL"

Holy Sparks
WWW.HOLYSPARKS.COM
©2020 Rae Shagalov

בס"ד

SOUL ADVENTURE #5

What is it like
to truly experience
THIS moment?
Let it land. ◉

ב"ה

How to be authentically yourself, while in a relationship with someone else.

I CAN SHOW THE MANY SIDES OF MYSELF, THE DARK AND THE LIGHT, AND KNOW THE OTHER WILL STILL LOVE ME.

THERE'S NO SUCH THING AS THE ONE AND ONLY ONE.

We don't have just one soulmate.

DEPENDING ON HOW MUCH WORK YOU'VE DONE ON YOURSELF, YOU WILL ATTRACT PEOPLE WHO HAVE DONE A SIMILAR AMOUNT OF WORK.

Going inward and making changes brings change in your relationships.

VULNERABILITY ALLOWS US TO GROW AND BECOME BETTER PEOPLE. VULNERABILITY WITH OURSELVES ALLOWS US TO GROW FROM ONE LEVEL TO A NEW LEVEL. THIS CREATES GEULA.

RABBI YISROEL BERNATH
SHIFRA CHANA HENDRIE

Geula is intimacy with G‑d.

Shalom Bayis, Peace in the home, brings Geula.

G‑d has a desire

G‑D WANTS US TO CREATE FOR HIM A DWELLING PLACE IN THESE LOWER REALMS. EVIL EXISTS TO GIVE US AN AUTHENTIC CHOICE TO MAKE THIS WORLD HOLY FOR G‑D. WHEN MOSHIACH COMES, EVIL WILL CEASE TO EXIST AND WE WILL LOSE THIS FREE CHOICE.

What is it like to truly experience THIS moment? Let it land.

"LOVE, RELATIONSHIPS, AND YOUR SOUL'S STORY"
Global Geula Summit
"CONVERSATIONS FROM THE EDGE OF HUMAN POTENTIAL"

Holy Sparks

בס"ד

SOUL ADVENTURE #6

How can you go out of
your comfort zone this week?

Holy
Sparks
©2020 Rae Shagalov
WWW.HOLYSPARKS.COM

Become a vessel for a blessing

IN ORDER TO RECEIVE A GREATER FLOW OF BLESSING, WE NEED TO BECOME A GREATER VESSEL OF SOUL TO RECEIVE IT.

Go out of your comfort zone.

SOMETIMES THE VESSEL WE HAVE IS FULL OF JUNK. SO, THE FIRST THING WE NEED TO DO IS EMPTY AND CLEAR IT OUT. HOW? WITH PHYSICAL MITZVAHS.

◆ GIVE A CERTAIN AMOUNT OF CHARITY EVERY DAY, AND A BIT MORE.

◆ MAKE SET TIMES FOR LEARNING CHASSIDUS EVERY DAY.

◆ CREATE AN EMOTIONAL VESSEL TO RECEIVE IT.

Ezer Kenegdo

A TRUE SOULMATE WILL LOVE YOU FOR WHO YOU ARE, LOVE YOU AND CHALLENGE YOU TO GROW, BECAUSE THEY LOVE YOU. YOU GROW TOGETHER, YOU KEEP GROWING YOUR AUTHENTIC SELF, AND SUPPORTING EACH OTHER, EVEN AS YOU ARE PUSHING AGAINST EACH OTHER.

RABBI YISROEL BERNATH
SHIFRA CHANA HENDRIE

WE ARE NOT MEANT TO BE ALONE.

ב"ה

Cut through your story to the center of who you are

IS THERE SPACE IN YOUR LIFE FOR SOMEONE ELSE? IS THERE SPACE IN YOUR LIFE FOR G-D? THIS WORLD IS NOT ABOUT COMFORT. IT'S ABOUT BEING REAL, CONNECTED, EMOTIONALLY VULNERABLE, RECEPTIVE.

when you change your identity, you change your mazel.

WHEN YOU BECOME A GREATER VESSEL FOR BLESSING, WHEN YOU CHANGE AND EXPAND THE LIMITS OF WHO YOU THINK YOU ARE, AND ENTER THE GREATER LEVEL OF SOUL TO BECOME WHO YOU TRULY ARE, YOU ENTER YOUR PERSONAL GEULA.

Geula is the process of self-rectification and liberation from the constraints of ego.

AND DIFFERENTIATING,

« LOVE, RELATIONSHIPS, AND YOUR SOUL'S STORY »
Global Geula Summit
" CONVERSATIONS FROM THE EDGE OF HUMAN POTENTIAL "

Holy Sparks

WWW.HOLYSPARKS.COM
©2020 Rae Shagalov

בס״ד

SOUL ADVENTURE #7

Record your next dream here.

A DREAM IS YOUR SUBCONSCIOUS SPEAKING TO YOU.

בס"ד

We begin and end our day with compassion.

AT NIGHT, WE SAY THE BEDTIME SHEMA. WE FORGIVE EVERYONE. WE DO A PERSONAL INVENTORY OF THE SOUL. WHAT DID WE DO RIGHT? WHAT DO WE NEED TO FIX AND CHANGE. WE WIPE OUR SLATE CLEAN, AND WHEN WE DO, IT BRINGS US TO A HIGHER LEVEL OF CONSCIOUSNESS WITHIN OURSELVES.

Ask for a dream.

Ask for a Divine message in your dreams.

Value your dreams.

Scary dreams

THESE ARE THE WARS THAT ARE GOING ON INSIDE OF US. OUR DREAMS COME TO HELP US FIGHT THE ENEMY INSIDE OF US, TO OVERCOME THE SCARY THINGS, AND WORK WITH THEM.

Keep a dream journal.

RECORD YOUR DREAMS AS SOON AS YOU WAKE UP. KEEP YOUR JOURNAL BY YOUR BED.

They are Divine messages directly to your soul.

WE ARE GIVEN WARNINGS IN OUR DREAMS, TO WORK THROUGH.

After the war, ask for the blessing.

FIGHT THE DREAM ENEMY AND ASK FOR A GIFT.

This Galus is a dream. When Geula comes, we will wake up from the dream of this world. BUT WE DON'T HAVE TO WAIT.

Our dreams come to heal us.

ALL DREAMS CAN BE INTERPRETED FOR THE GOOD.

We can wake up NOW!

Holy Sparks

CHAYA LESTER
SHIFRA CHANA HENDRIE
"PROPHECY AND THE POWER OF YOUR DREAMS"
Global Geula Summit
"CONVERSATIONS FROM THE EDGE OF HUMAN POTENTIAL"

SOUL ADVENTURE #8

Which of the many facets of Torah awakens your heart the most?

Holy Sparks

Which of the many facets of Torah awakens your heart the most?

Our miracles begin in our heart

A Tree Meditation

PLANT YOUR FEET ON THE GROUND LIKE A ROOTED TREE. SEND YOUR ROOTS DOWN TO GROUND INTO ADAMA, THE EARTH. CONNECT DEEPLY TO YOUR VISION THROUGH YOUR IMAGINATION. LET THE ENERGY RISE FROM THE GROUND INTO YOU, INTO YOUR HEART, WARMING IT SWEETLY. RISING HIGHER INTO THE FRUIT OF A WORD, A PRAYER, A LONGING...

G‑d is calling for our participation in making this world holy.

Torah is the means of a quest, a journey of unfolding discovery, of the oneness of G‑d.

WE ARE ALL AIMING FOR THE SAME INFINITE TRUTH.

When we listen carefully, we can hear the underlying melody of the song that is being sung through us. AT THE HEART OF THE TREE, THE WATERS SWEETEN INTO AN EXPRESSION—A FRUIT, A THOUGHT, A WORD.

Don't expect, Aspire!

ENVISION FROM WITHIN YOUR HEART. REPLACE EXPECTATIONS WITH YEARNING.

"DIVINE CONTACT PRAYER: TOUCHING WHOLENESS, DRAWING BLESSING, CREATING PEACE"
RAV DANIEL KOHN ◆ SHIFRA CHANA HENDRIE

Global Geula Summit

"CONVERSATIONS FROM THE EDGE OF HUMAN POTENTIAL"

Holy Sparks

בס"ד

SOUL ADVENTURE #9

In what area of your life can you move your ego
out of the way to make room for G-d?

How can I move my ego out of the way so the revelation of G-d can flow through me so that I can touch that Infinity?

But still retain my uniqueness?

G-D WANTS TO BE REVEALED IN THIS FINITE WORLD. G-D WANTS US TO REVEAL THE INFINITE PART OF OURSELVES IN OUR FINITE SELF, REMOVING THE THINGS THAT BLOCK OUR INFINITE SELVES.

We are rooted in the ground of reality while we branch out, grow, and reach for the Infinite.

THE SAP RISES. THE SONG EMERGES.

Inspired from that place in between...

Open to G-d but still uniquely you

FROM THE SPECIFIC TO THE UNIVERSAL AND BACK TO THE SPECIFIC.

MAY OUR NEW VISION BE GROUNDED IN OUR REALNESS AS WE REACH UPWARD WITH OUR YEARNING FOR OUR FULLER, REALIZED PERFECTION IN OURSELVES AND OUTWARD TO THOSE WE ARE CONNECTED TO THROUGHOUT HUMANITY.

"DIVINE CONTACT PRAYER: TOUCHING WHOLENESS, DRAWING BLESSING, CREATING PEACE"
RAV DANIEL KOHN ◆ SHIFRA CHANA HENDRIE
Global Geula Summit
"CONVERSATIONS FROM THE EDGE OF HUMAN POTENTIAL"

Holy Sparks
WWW.HOLYSPARKS.COM
©2020 Rae Shagalov

SOUL ADVENTURE #10

How can you be more fully
and uniquely who you are?

What does Redemption look like? ב"ה

THE TORAH LOOKS AT LIFE FROM ALL PERSPECTIVES.

It's time to be fully who you are!

WHEN YOU FIND THE SPIRITUALITY IN THE PHYSICALITY, THEN YOU CAN BRING THE PHYSICALITY INTO SPIRITUALITY.

Mazel

WHEN YOU CHANGE YOUR NEGATIVE PAST, YOU CHANGE YOUR MAZEL.

We can't see there from here.

Torah wisdom is meant to transform the physical world.

Right NOW, in everything we do.

WHEN THE JEWS ARE AWESOME IN TORAH, THE WORLD WANTS TO COME ALONG.

WE'RE MEANT TO LIVE TORAH WISDOM IN REAL TIME.

We expect the past to look a lot like the future. We have no idea what the messianic era will really be like. We just know the Torah is the blueprint to get us there.

EVERY STAGE OF GEULAH IS A LOCKED DOOR... UNTIL YOU UNLOCK IT. WE KEEP TRANSFORMING AND PROGRESSING. WE'RE NEVER DONE IN OUR SERVICE TO G-D. THERE'S ALWAYS ANOTHER CHALLENGE, THERE'S ALWAYS SOMETHING MORE BECAUSE G-D IS INFINITE. YOU CAN'T DICTATE WHERE G-D IS TAKING YOU. GET COMFORTABLE WITH THE UNKNOWN.

Everyone struggles with something.

RABBI DAVID KATZ — "THE PATH OF THE GER: THE FUTURE TORAH EMERGING THROUGH YOU"

SHIFRA CHANA HENDRIE — "AWAKENING THE SOUL OF HUMANITY"

Global Geula Summit
"CONVERSATIONS FROM THE EDGE OF HUMAN POTENTIAL"

Holy Sparks

ב"ה

SOUL ADVENTURE #11

UNLOCK THE NEXT LEVEL OF INFINITY!

What is something you are denying or avoiding?
What is one step you could take to face the truth of it?

בס"ד

Be true to your principles and ideals. Torah is simple once you listen to its sublime, pristine message.

THE REBBE

Open your eyes

GET USED TO A LIFE OF: THIS IS UNEXPECTED, AS USUAL.

TO SEE MOSHIACH AND THE UNFOLDING OF GEULAH. ONE OF THE KEYS TO GEULAH IS TO Be fully invested in the PRESENT MOMENT.

IF YOU LEARN SOMETHING IN TORAH THAT SEEMS TO CONTRADICT WHAT YOU THINK YOU KNOW TO BE TRUE, IT IS ONLY BECAUSE YOU HAVEN'T LEARNED TORAH DEEPLY ENOUGH YET. WHEN YOU DO, THE CONTRADICTION FALLS AWAY.

You're not doomed and you're not cursed.

THE NATURE OF THE TRUTH IS THAT IT'S RIGHT IN FRONT OF YOU.

Bring in the full context.

Living a Torah life changes your mazel and lifts you above.

NO ONE IS LEFT OUT OF TORAH. IT'S THE BLUEPRINT OF ALL OF CREATION.

There's always something to face.

HAVE THE COURAGE TO READ AND INVESTIGATE UNTIL WHAT YOU ARE DENYING OR AVOIDING IS SO PROFOUNDLY REVEALED IN TRUTH IN FRONT OF YOU THAT YOU CANNOT DENY IT ANY MORE.

This is how to unlock the next level of growth, of infinity.

RABBI DAVID KATZ
SHIFRA CHANA HENDRIE

"THE PATH OF THE GER: AWAKENING THE SOUL OF HUMANITY"

"THE FUTURE TORAH EMERGING THROUGH YOU"

Holy Sparks

Global Geula Summit

"CONVERSATIONS FROM THE EDGE OF HUMAN POTENTIAL"

SOUL ADVENTURE #12

STEP TO THE END OF THE PARADOX!

What is one thing you can give your all to
and push yourself to the limits of your self?
Plan it out below.

Ask G-d to help you and let it go!

בס"ד

We have to master every day living before we can master transcendent living.

WHEN YOU BUILD, AND ALIGN, AND PERFECT YOUR CONSCIOUSNESS, THIS IS MENTAL HEALTH. YOUR BELIEFS ALIGN WITH YOUR HEART, YOUR HEART ALIGNS WITH YOUR VALUES, YOUR BODY, TRAINING, AND HABITS ALIGN WITH YOUR HIGHEST, DEEPEST WILL. THEN YOU CAN **LET GO** and LET G-D. THEN SOMETHING MORE AND DEEPER CAN COME THROUGH YOU.

Our responsibility is to harness and align lower self IN MARRIAGE, WORK, RELATIONSHIPS, OUR CRAFT, OUR TEACHING to develop the vessel of who we are, in order to channel G-dliness through us, into this world.

when we let go and trust G-d, that's when the Blessing comes.

WHEN WE DO THE BEST WE CAN WITH WHO WE ARE, AND WHAT WE HAVE, AND THEN GIVE IT OVER TO G-D, G-D WILL TAKE US THAT LAST STEP HIGHER AND DEEPER THAN WE EVER THOUGHT POSSIBLE.

This is how to make the two worlds Kiss THE UPPER WORLD AND THE LOWER WORLD.

You have to walk to the end of the paradox.

HOW MUCH SHOULD I DO? HOW MUCH SHOULD I LET GO AND TRUST IN G-D?

where do I begin and G-d ends? YOU HAVE TO BE WILLING TO STEP UP TO THE THRESHOLD AND GIVE YOUR ALL UNTIL YOU REACH THE LIMITS OF YOUR SELF. THEN YOU BECOME AN EMPTY VESSEL THAT CAN RECEIVE EVERYTHING. THIS IS MALKHUS.

THIS IS HOW WE CAN GIVE GIFTS TO THE WORLD THAT ARE GREATER THAN WHO WE ARE.

Holy Sparks
WWW.HOLYSPARKS.COM
©2020 Rae Shagalov

RAV DONIEL KATZ
SHIFRA CHANA HENDRIE
"SECRETS OF DIVINE CONSCIOUSNESS" "CONVERSATIONS FROM THE EDGE OF HUMAN POTENTIAL"

Global Geula Summit

בס"ד

SOUL
ADVENTURE
#13

What is a way you could share
something about G-d with other people?

בס"ד

Your humility opens yourself up to that which is beyond yourself.

WE ARE SUPPOSED TO EMBODY THE TRUTH OURSELVES, WITH LIGHT, LOVE, AND COMPASSION, AND SHARE THAT BEYOND OURSELVES WITH THE WORLD.

When you reach the end of self, then you can go beyond the limits of your self.

You have to realize that you are loved and you are blessed. You are safe and connected, and G-d is with you, and in all things.

REMEMBER THIS WHEN YOU GO THROUGH THE CHALLENGES AND THE MIRACLES.

RAV DONIEL KATZ
SHIFRA CHANA HENDRIE
"SECRETS OF DIVINE CONSCIOUSNESS"
Global Geula Summit
"CONVERSATIONS FROM THE EDGE OF HUMAN POTENTIAL"

There is no reality other than G-d.

THE GOAL IS THAT EVERY HUMAN BEING IS AWARE OF THIS, UNTIL THE WHOLE WORLD IS FULL OF DIVINE CONSCIOUSNESS.

It's our responsibility to share this with the world.

Holy Sparks

בס"ד

SOUL ADVENTURE #14

What do you think is your strongest talent?
How can you shine it even brighter?

Shine your light into the world...

You're going to be everything and yourself at the same time.

YOU WILL HAVE A SEPARATE SELF, A LOWER CONSCIOUSNESS, BUT IT WILL BE SO UNIFIED AND HARMONIZED IN GEULAH, THERE WILL BE NO CONTRADICTION BETWEEN YOUR HIGHER CONSCIOUSNESS AND YOUR LOWER CONSCIOUSNESS.

ב"ה

YOU ARE A UNIQUE ESSENTIAL, IRREPLACABLE, GORGEOUS, PRECIOUS, NECESSARY EXPRESSION OF THE DIVINE UNITY OF G-D! YES- YOU!

Our true selves will unify with G-d.

WE ARE EXPANDING INTO G-D'S REALITY, RIGHT HERE, RIGHT NOW!

Shine your light into the world.
The world of separateness will unify completely.

YOUR EXPRESSION OF YOUR OWN G-DLINESS SHINES AND ILLUMINATES MY G-DLINESS.

THE TREE OF LIFE WAS EMBEDDED INSIDE OF THE TREE OF KNOWLEDGE, JUST AS THE GEULAH IS EMBEDDED INSIDE OF THE GALUS, JUST AS THE HIGHER SELF IS EMBEDDED INSIDE OF THE PERSONAL STRUGGLING SELF. EVERYTHING EXISTS ALREADY PERFECT.

Our consciousness affects reality.

The Paradox:

① MOSHIACH CAN COME AT ANY MOMENT.
② IT'S TOTALLY DEPENDENT ON ME.
① THERE IS MUCH WORK TO DO.
② THE WORK IS ALREADY DONE.

NOT ONLY WILL WE BE BACK IN THE GARDEN OF EDEN WHEN MOSHIACH COMES, WE WILL REALIZE THAT WE WERE THERE ALL ALONG! WE ARE THE GARDENERS. WE CHERISHED AND BUILT GEULAH WITH OUR HUMBLE EFFORTS.

Shabbos reminds us that the work is already completed.

There isn't any other place than right here, and there isn't any other time than right now.

Holy Sparks

RAV DONIEL KATZ
SHIFRA CHANA HENDRIE **Global Geula Summit** "CONVERSATIONS FROM THE EDGE OF HUMAN POTENTIAL"
"SECRETS OF DIVINE CONSCIOUSNESS"

WWW.HOLYSPARKS.COM ©2020 Rae Shagalov

SOUL ADVENTURE #15

What Holy Sparks in your life do you need to elevate?
How can you elevate them to bring Geulah into them?

בס"ד

Open your eyes and see that the whole world is a miracle! IT'S NOT NATURE. IT'S MIRACLE! NATURE CONCEALS THE G-DLINESS. THE WHOLE WORLD IS DIVINE REVELATION. THE GEULAH REVELATION IS TO BE ABLE TO SEE THE G-DLINESS IN ALL THINGS, AT ALL TIMES.

Open up and let the light of Geulah flow through YOU!

Geulah is already present! Right Here. Right NOW. Dig in!

This is the age of integration. It's all coming together in our generation.

We look for the Holy Sparks to elevate in the darkest parts of our experience. DON'T SUPPRESS OR NEGATE THE DARKEST PARTS OF YOUR LIFE. EMBRACE THEM AND REVEAL THE LIGHT WITHIN THEM.

Look deeply inside of yourself and bring out your inner light from there, where you are unified with G-d and all souls. YOU HAVE TO LIVE TORAH ALL THE WAY DEEP INTO YOUR KISHKES.

SEE YOUR STRUGGLES IN THE LIGHT OF THE DIVINE. G-D IS EVERYWHERE, EVEN IN YOUR DARKNESS.

We're all going to get there together, each doing our own unique work, fulfilling our individual missions. YOUR FEAR, YOUR EGO, YOUR NEGATIVITY HAS TREMENDOUS LIGHT WITHIN IT. IT'S JUST BEING MIS-CHANNELED. ALL HEALING COMES WHEN WE TURN ON THE LIGHT IN THE DARKNESS. WE DON'T NEGATE DARKNESS, WE DON'T DESTROY DARKNESS.

We turn on the light in our darkness. The Garden of Eden is inside of us.

RAV DONIEL KATZ
SHIFRA CHANA HENDRIE
"SECRETS OF DIVINE CONSCIOUSNESS"
Global Geula Summit
"CONVERSATIONS FROM THE EDGE OF HUMAN POTENTIAL"

Holy Sparks
WWW.HOLYSPARKS.COM
©2020 Rae Shagalov

בס״ד

SOUL ADVENTURE #16

Where in your life do you need
to increase your awareness of G-d?
What can you do to remember the G-dliness there?

Deeper and deeper awareness of G‑d within our own every day reality is where we touch Infinity. This is the Infinity we can reach from where we are.

HOLINESS RADIATES THROUGH YOU!

Shine your light into the world.

ENVISION A LIGHT COMING DOWN FROM THE INFINITE LIGHT INTO YOUR HIGHER CONSCIOUSNESS, INTO YOUR MIND, INTO YOUR HEART, THE LIGHT OF LOVE AND THE LIGHT OF STRUCTURE AND VESSELS SHINING BETWEEN YOUR HANDS. FEEL THE ENERGY OF THAT LIGHT BETWEEN YOUR HANDS AND POINT IT AT YOUR HEART, OPENING AND EXPANDING YOUR HEART.

THINK OF A MOMENT IN YOUR LIFE WHEN YOU EXPERIENCED TREMENDOUS LOVE. LIVE IN THE EXPERIENCE AND RELIVE THE MOST POTENT MOMENT OF CONNECTION. CHOOSE ANOTHER MOMENT OF LOVE AND RELIVE IT, IN VIBRANT DETAIL. CHOOSE A MEMORY OF HOLINESS, A MOMENT OF TRANSCENDENCE, A SPIRITUAL EXPERIENCE, MORE THAN YOURSELF, AT ONE WITH THE UNIVERSE. RELIVE IT.

In Geulah

THERE WON'T BE ANY MORE SICKNESS. THERE WON'T BE ANY MORE DEATH. THERE WON'T BE POVERTY, STRUGGLE, JEALOUSY.

We'll live forever occupied with Knowing G‑d.

EVERYTHING WILL BE AVAILABLE INFINITELY, ALL OF THE PHYSICAL PLEASURES, AND EMOTIONAL PLEASURES, AND SPIRITUAL PLEASURES, BUT THE GREATEST PLEASURE OF ALL WILL BE KNOWING G‑D, AND WE'LL NEVER RUN OUT OF G‑D TO KNOW!

Sometimes we get a glimpse of a deeper reality.

EVERY MITZVAH, EVERY HALACHA GIVES US A GLIMPSE OF THE DIVINE REALITY.

The experience of the One of Unity is the experience of love.

THE POWER OF GEULAH IS THE UNIFICATION OF ALL THINGS: HEAVEN AND EARTH, MIND AND HEART, BODY AND SOUL, JEWS AND NON-JEWS. ERETZ YISRAEL EXPANDS OUT INTO THE WORLD.

There is deep hope and pleasure to connect to the One, to Know and be Known.

THE BROKENNESS IS ALSO G‑D, WE CHOSE TO STEP OUT OF THE GARDEN. WE CAN CHOOSE TO STEP BACK INTO THE GARDEN.

EACH OF THESE MOMENTS IS A GIFT FROM G‑D TO GIVE A TASTE OF GEULAH.

RELIVE THE FIRST MEMORY OF LOVE, THEN THE SECOND MEMORY OF LOVE, THEN THE MOMENT OF HOLINESS. BACK TO THE FIRST MEMORY OF LOVE AND SEE THE HOLINESS IN THE LOVE AND FEEL THE LOVE IN THE HOLINESS.

Global Geula Summit

RAV DONIEL KATZ
SHIFRA CHANA HENDRIE
"SECRETS OF DIVINE CONSCIOUSNESS"

"CONVERSATIONS FROM THE EDGE OF HUMAN POTENTIAL"

Holy Sparks

בס"ד

Shine your light and your love into the world.

Choose and believe that we are all connected, one heart and one soul.

G-D GAVE YOU MOMENTS OF INFINITE LOVE AND INFINITE HOLINESS SO THAT THE WHOLE WORLD, AND ALL PEOPLE, AND ANIMALS, VEGETABLES, MINERALS, ALL OF THE CITIES AND ALL OF THE COUNTRIES WILL RECEIVE THAT LIGHT AND REVELATION THAT RADIATES FROM YOU. ASK G-D TO FLOOD THE WORLD WITH EXPANDED EMUNAH. CONNECT TO THE HOLINESS OF THE LAND OF ISRAEL AND THE HOLY OF HOLIES. CHANNEL THE LIGHT FROM THERE TO HERE AND EVERYWHERE, FLOOD THE WORLD WITH THAT LIGHT AND HEALING.

OPEN YOUR HEART TO MIRACLES, THAT TRANSFORMATION IS POSSIBLE, THAT HEALING & SALVATION IS POSSIBLE. DRAW THE LIGHT OF GEULAH INTO THE WORLD AND INTO YOURSELF. ASK G-D FOR GEULAH WITH A SMILE, A SIMPLE REQUEST, AND A TRUSTING HEART. KEEP GOING HIGHER AND HIGHER!

Choose to receive love and light, blessing and holiness from everyone because we are all interconnected. Choose and believe and that faith alone will enable you to receive that love and light.

HEALING DOESN'T HAVE TO BE HARSH & STRUGGLING, IT CAN BE ALLOWING AND RECEIVING.

May all the goodness of the world be revealed!

RAV DONIEL KATZ
SHIFRA CHANA HENDRIE
"SECRETS OF DIVINE CONSCIOUSNESS"

Global Geula Summit
"CONVERSATIONS FROM THE EDGE OF HUMAN POTENTIAL"

Holy Sparks
WWW.HOLYSPARKS.COM
©2020 Rae Shagalov

ב"ה

When we fulfill the purpose of the challenge, the light is revealed.

SOUL ADVENTURE #17

What is one of your challenges?
What do you think is its Divine purpose?
How can you bring the light out of it?

Your challenges contain a deeper light that's embedded in the darkness, so profound, it can only be revealed through the challenges.

When we fulfill the purpose of the challenge, the light is revealed.

If G☀d loves us so much, why is life so hard?

TO HELP US DEVELOP OUR RELATIONSHIP WITH OUR CREATOR, WHO IS ALWAYS WITH US, ALWAYS SUPPORTING US, ALWAYS INVITING US TO CONNECT TO HIM.

HAYA BAKER
SHIFRA CHANA HENDRIE
"HEALING BODY AND SOUL"
Global Geula Summit
"CONVERSATIONS FROM THE EDGE OF HUMAN POTENTIAL"

בס"ד

Be real with G☀d.
G☀d can handle it.

WE KNOW THAT WE ARE LIGHT BEINGS DEEP INSIDE AND WE FEEL ASHAMED BECAUSE WE ARE IN A DIMINISHED FORM, NOT LIVING UP TO OUR POTENTIAL. WHEN WE ARE WILLING TO EXPERIENCE OUR DIMINISHMENT AND OUR HUMAN LIMITATIONS WITHIN THE EMBRACE OF OUR LOVING CREATOR, OUR CREATOR HELPS US OPEN THE GATES OF THE GARDEN OF EDEN TO ALL THE LIGHT WITHIN.

G☀d is seeking to connect to you.

Put your hand over your heart and hold yourself in compassion. Accept yourself with your struggle.

Holy Sparks

WWW.HOLYSPARKS.COM
©2020 Rae Shagalov

בס"ד

WHERE ARE YOU?

ACKNOWLEDGE WITH COMPASSION WHERE YOU ARE, WHAT YOU'RE GOING THROUGH, AND WHAT'S TRUE FOR YOU.

SOUL ADVENTURE #18

Set a timer for 5 minutes.
Ask yourself, "Where are you?" Write the answer.
Repeat until the timer signals you to stop.

ב"ה

Allow the Creator to breathe through you and caress all of the constricted places within you, with unconditional love and honor for your experience, and your dedication, in spite of all difficulties, and for your sacrifice, and for the pain you still endure, with complete acceptance.

WHENEVER YOU ARE STRUGGLING, RECONNECT TO YOUR HEART, OBSERVE WITH YOUR MIND, AND BREATHE THROUGH YOUR BODY, TO ENLIVEN EVERY ORGAN, EVERY TISSUE, BREATHE YOUR JOY, LOVE, AND SERENITY THROUGHOUT YOUR BODY TO NOURISH EVERY CELL, EVERY SYSTEM.

G‑d renews you every moment.

You are not alone. Your Creator is with you in your pain.

WHERE ARE YOU?

ACKNOWLEDGE WITH COMPASSION WHERE YOU ARE, WHAT YOU'RE GOING THROUGH, AND WHAT'S TRUE FOR YOU.

WE ARE ENTERING A TIME WHEN THE STRUGGLE — OUR STRUGGLES WITHIN — WILL OPEN THE GATE TO THE GARDEN OF EDEN. IT WILL SOON OPEN UP TO THE ULTIMATE REALITY.

SINCE HEAVEN KISSED EARTH AT SINAI, THERE HAS BEEN A GLIMMER OF LIGHT THAT'S GROWING.

May you always feel the love of your Creator.

HAYA BAKER
SHIFRA CHANA HENDRIE
"HEALING BODY AND SOUL"

Holy Sparks

Global Geula Summit

"CONVERSATIONS FROM THE EDGE OF HUMAN POTENTIAL"

WWW.HOLYSPARKS.COM
©2020 Rae Shagalov

בס"ד

SOUL ADVENTURE #19

How can you spread holiness today?

Holy Sparks www.HOLYSPARKS.com ©2020 Rae Shagalov

54

Geulah is so incredibly beyond what we know, we can not even understand what it is.

GEULAH IS NOT JUST AN ABSENCE OF DEATH, HUNGER, ILLNESS, WAR, ETC. JUST AS AN UNBORN BABY CAN'T IMAGINE WHAT HIS LIFE WILL BE.

The Birthpangs of Moshiach.

THE TRANSITIONAL FIGURE IS:

Moshiach Ben Yosef
REMOVES THE EVIL OF THE WORLD.

Moshiach Ben David
BRINGS DOWN THE KEDUSHA IN GEULAH, THE HOLINESS, THE BAIS HAMIKDASH, THE TEMPLE, AND AWESOME SPIRITUALITY.

Why does G‑d allow evil to proliferate?

TO DEMONSTRATE HIS TREMENDOUS POWER IN THE END OF DAYS. G‑D INCREASES THE DARKNESS SO THAT WE AND HE CAN REVEAL THE TREMENDOUS LIGHT OF GEULAH, AND THE ABSOLUTE POWER OF G‑D.

ב"ה

We are meant to spread Holiness, TO SUBDUE EVIL AND DESTROY IT.

To remind the world there is nothing else but G‑d. EVERYTHING EMANATES FROM G‑D.

To reveal the reality of G‑d.

Moshiach transforms the fabric of the world.

THE JEWISH PEOPLE ARE THE BEARERS OF SPIRITUALITY. WE TEACH THE ONENESS OF G‑D. OUR UNIQUE MISSION AS JEWS ALLOWS THE PRESENCE OF G‑D TO RE-ENTER CREATION.

This is the tikkun, the fixing of the world.

The Exodus from Egypt is the model of Redemption.

RABBI MENDEL KESSIN
SHIFRA CHANA HENDRIE

"SIGNS OF REDEMPTION PROPHECY, CHAOS & CURRENT EVENTS"

Global Geula Summit

"CONVERSATIONS FROM THE EDGE OF HUMAN POTENTIAL"

Holy Sparks
WWW.HOLYSPARKS.COM
©2020 Rae Shagalov

ב"ה

This is the last battle between good and evil

We are in the Messianic Era now, and it is progressing swiftly

WE HAVE THE PRIVILEGE OF TAKING A PEEK BEHIND THE CURTAIN AS WE SEE THE DRAMA UNFOLDING AND UNDERSTAND HOW IT FITS WITH THE TORAH'S INNER STORY.

The Divine Plan is rapidly unfolding

The Erev Rav

ARE JEWISH LEADERS WHO UNFORTUNATELY WANT TO BREAK THE UNIQUE SPIRITUAL BOND BETWEEN THE JEWS AND OUR CREATOR. THE EREV RAV ARE SOLDIERS OF THE SATAN, DESTROYING THE JEWISH PEOPLE FROM WITHIN BY EATING AWAY JEWISH SPIRITUALITY. THEY LEAD THE JEWS AWAY FROM THE HOLINESS OF TORAH BY HIDING BEHIND THEIR JEWISHNESS. THE EREV RAV PROLONGS THE SUFFERING OF THE JEWS. THEIR TIME IS SOON OVER.

The purpose of antisemitism is also to test the nations of the world.

WHEN ANTISEMITISM ARISES IN YOUR COUNTRY, IN YOUR CITY, WHAT ARE YOU GOING TO DO ABOUT IT? ARE YOU GOING TO PROTECT YOUR JEWS, G-D'S CHILDREN THAT WERE ENTRUSTED TO YOUR CARE?

DEVARIM

"Even if your exiles are at the end of Heaven, from there I will gather you and take you to Me."

THIS IS A DIVINE PROMISE THAT NO MATTER WHERE THEY HAVE BEEN SCATTERED ALL OVER THE EARHT, ALL JEWS WILL RETURN. G-D WILL BRING ALL HIS KIDS BACK.

RABBI MENDEL KESSIN "SIGNS OF REDEMPTION
SHIFRA CHANA HENDRIE PROPHECY, CHAOS & CURRENT EVENTS"

Global Geula Summit

"CONVERSATIONS FROM THE EDGE OF HUMAN POTENTIAL"

Holy Sparks
WWW.HOLYSPARKS.COM
©2020 Rae Shagalov

בס"ד

There is a Moshiach for every generation who is the root soul.

The rectification of the world is 99% complete.

PHASE ONE:
The footsteps of the Moshiach

MOSHIACH IS SO CLOSE YOU COULD SEE HIS FOOTSTEPS IN THE GROUND. THAT STARTED IN 1840. WE ARE IN ACT 3, SCENE 3 ⊘ THE PLOT NO LONGER NEEDS TO BE DEVELOPED. WE ARE IN THE CLIMAX OF THE CREATION STORY. WE ARE NOW BEING PREPARED FOR THE MESSIANIC AGE.

PHASE TWO:
The beginning of Redemption

THE ENTRANCE OF MOSHIACH BEN YOSEF WHO WILL BE GREATER THAN ABRAHAM, GREATER THAN MOSHE RABBEINU, GREATER THAN ANGELS

The world will be filled with the knowledge of G·d.

MOSHIACH BEN YOSEF WILL GROW AND G-D WILL ALLOW THE JEWISH PEOPLE TO GROW WITH HIM. MOSHIACH WILL SUFFER GREATLY SO THAT THE JEWISH PEOPLE AND THE WORLD CAN BE REHABILITATED.

We are in this world to subdue evil and bring Holiness down

MOSHIACH'S SUFFERING ATONES FOR OUR SINS. MOSHIACH BEN YOSEF'S JOB IS TO TAKE ON THE NATIONS OF THE WORLD AND REBUILD THE HOLY TEMPLE.

"Let that which is yours be yours.

ESAV RETURNS IN THE END OF TIME TO REPENT AND ASSIST YAAKOV AND THE JEWISH PEOPLE BY RESTORING THE BIRTHRIGHT TO THE LAND OF ISRAEL AND PROTECTING THE JEWS FROM THEIR ENEMIES.

RABBI MENDEL KESSIN   "SIGNS OF REDEMPTION
SHIFRA CHANA HENDRIE   PROPHECY, CHAOS & CURRENT EVENTS"

Global Geula Summit
"CONVERSATIONS FROM THE EDGE OF HUMAN POTENTIAL"

Holy Sparks

57

SOUL ADVENTURE #20

בס״ד

What do you need to do
to prepare yourself for Geulah?
Which of your priorities need to shift?

How To Prepare for the Rapidly Unfolding Geulah

ב"ה

① Begin and intensify your spiritual journey.

AFTER MOSHIACH COMES THERE WILL BE NO MORE FREE CHOICE BECAUSE THE WHOLE WORLD WILL BE FULL OF THE REVELATION OF G-D. THERE WILL BE NO MORE OPPORTUNITY FOR TESHUVA, BECAUSE EVERYONE WILL SEE THE TRUTH OF EVERYTHING.

change your priorities NOW.

② Be careful NOT to harm others.

BE KIND. BE GENTLE. BE MERCIFUL.

TREAT OTHERS THE WAY YOU WANT G-D TO TREAT YOU. G-D WANTS BROTHERHOOD AND SISTERHOOD. FOCUS ON PROSPERITY FOR ALL INSTEAD OF THE NEED TO CONQUER.

Cultivate Kindness.

③ Don't Gossip or Slander.

WHEN YOU SPEAK NEGATIVELY ABOUT OTHERS, YOU ARE JUDGED NEGATIVELY ON HIGH.

we create the world through our speech, just as G-d did.

④ Look for G-d in everything.

Don't wait Start NOW.

RABBI MENDEL KESSIN "SIGNS OF REDEMPTION
SHIFRA CHANA HENDRIE PROPHECY, CHAOS & CURRENT EVENTS"
Global Geula Summit
"CONVERSATIONS FROM THE EDGE OF HUMAN POTENTIAL"

Holy Sparks

WWW.HOLYSPARKS.COM
©2020 Rae Shagalov

בס"ד

SOUL ADVENTURE #21

Think of something you need.
Who do you know who needs that same thing?
Pray for that person and do something to help them.

Holy Sparks
WWW.HOLYSPARKS.COM
©2020 Rae Shagalov

Prior to Light G‑d created the world of Tohu, chaos. THAT WORLD BROKE APART AND WAS RECONSTRUCTED AS THE WORLD OF TIKKUN, THE WORLD OF RECTIFICATION / OUR WORLD. WHY DID THE WORLD OF TOHU SHATTER? IT WAS BUILT TO SHATTER, IN ORDER TO RECTIFY AND REINTEGRATE THE WORLD, THROUGH THE WORK OF MAN. G‑D CREATED THIS WORLD TO BE PERFECTED BY US.

This is called the breaking of the vessels.

Devekut is a complete harmony and oneness with the essence of 'one's soul which is bound up with G‑d.

ב"ה

G‑d wants us to bring the highest level of G‑dliness to this world, through our avodah.

G‑D WANTS US TO REPAIR THE SHATTERED VESSELS OF THIS WORLD THROUGH OUR HARD WORK, AND TO BRING BACK THE ORIGINAL LIGHT OF CREATION THAT WAS LOST WHEN THE VESSELS SHATTERED.

The worlds devolved from higher to lower. THE WORLD OF TIKKUN DEVOLVED TO CAPTURE THE LOWEST HOLY SPARKS.

When you need help, help someone else. When you need prayers, pray for someone else who needs the same thing you do. This opens the channel of Blessing for both of you.

RABBI MOSHE MILLER
SHIFRA CHANA HENDRIE
"THE SPIRITUAL STRUCTURE OF THE UNIVERSE: EXPANDING THE RELATIONSHIP BETWEEN MAN, GOD & WORLD"

Global Geula Summit
"CONVERSATIONS FROM THE EDGE OF HUMAN POTENTIAL"

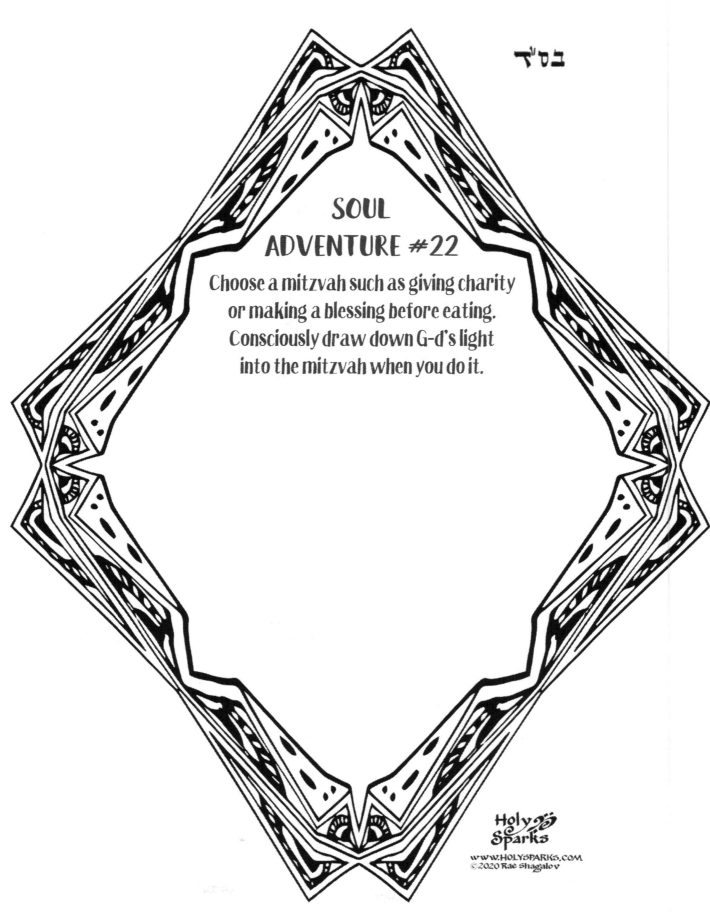

בס"ד

SOUL ADVENTURE #22

Choose a mitzvah such as giving charity or making a blessing before eating. Consciously draw down G-d's light into the mitzvah when you do it.

Holy Sparks
www.HOLYSPARKS.COM
©2020 Rae Shagalov

בס"ד

BAAL SHEM TOV

Now is the time to reveal the G-dliness in the multiplicities, grasping and revealing the Divine Unity in all things.

DEVEKUT: CLEAVING TO G-D

Chassidic Alchemy is transforming darkness into light.

ARIZAL

Yechudim Unifications
A DRAWING DOWN OF ENERGY FROM ABOVE TO BELOW, AND MERGING THROUGH INTERINCLUSION INTO A 3RD ENTITY, BRINGING THE HIGHER WORLD AND THE LOWER WORLD TOGETHER.

—EXODUS 23:5
"IF YOU SEE THE DONKEY OF YOUR ENEMY STRUGGLING UNDER ITS LOAD, HELP YOUR ENEMY." THE BAAL SHEM TOV EXPLAINS, WHEN YOU SEE YOUR DONKEY, YOUR ANIMAL SOUL STRUGGLING TO COME TO A SPIRITUAL ILLUMINATION, DON'T STRUGGLE WITH THE ANIMAL URGE. DON'T SMASH IT APART. INSTEAD, WORK WITH IT. USE IT TO GET TO A HIGHER LEVEL.

We are peeling away layers of reality to reveal TRUTH.

ANY ANGUISH AND SUFFERING IS AN OPPORTUNITY TO REACH FOR A SOURCE OF LIGHT.

Everything is G-dliness.
WHEN YOU NOTICE AND EXTRACT THE G-DLINESS IN EVERYTHING, YOU BRING GEULAH.

Everything comes from the same Source.

RAMAK

Kavanah Intention
IS MAKING A CHANNEL IN THE PHYSICAL, THE WAY IT IS IN REALITY, DRAWING DOWN G-DLINESS WITH INTENTION INTO THE ACTION OR PHYSICAL OBJECT OF THE MITZVAH. THIS DRAWS DIVINE LIGHT DOWN THROUGH THE SPIRITUAL WORLDS INTO THIS LOW PHYSICAL WORLD.

Everything is from G-d.. It's all part of G-d's Oneness.
IF YOU SEE EVEN THE LAYERS ARE G-DLINESS, THEN THE G-DLINESS WITHIN YOU BECOMES REVEALED.

Things that conceal the truth are part of the truth.

Holy Sparks
WWW.HOLYSPARKS.COM
©2020 Rae Shagalov

Global Geula Summit
"CONVERSATIONS FROM THE EDGE OF HUMAN POTENTIAL"

RABBI MOSHE MILLER
SHIFRA CHANA HENDRIE
"THE SPIRITUAL STRUCTURE OF THE UNIVERSE: EXPANDING THE RELATIONSHIP BETWEEN MAN, GOD & WORLD"

בס"ד

SOUL ADVENTURE #23

Set a timer for 5 minutes. Ask yourself,
"What does G-d want from me?" Write the answer.
Repeat until the timer signals you to stop.

בס"ד

EVERYTHING HAS A PURPOSE.

EVERYTHING IS MADE OF G-DLINESS.

DON'T RESIST AND RUN AWAY FROM THE HIDDEN G-DLINESS.

Reveal the hidden light of G-d in your life. ◆

Sometimes we feel like running and hiding...

Run toward what G-d wants!

In every situation, figure out what G-d wants. Run toward it with enthusiasm and that will immediately start changing the situation in a positive direction.

"NOTHING IS RANDOM."

"G-D LOVES ME."

"EVERYTHING IS FOR MY GOOD."

"EVERYTHING IS G-D."

"EVERYTHING IS POSSIBLE TO TRANSFORM."

EVERY TIME WE MAKE THIS DEEPER CONNECTION, IT DRILLS DOWN TO THE CORE OF CREATION AND RADIATES OUT THROUGH TIME AND SPACE.

נִסָיוֹן

TEST
MIRACLE
BANNER

The trial contains within itself the miracle of success to lift yourself up to a higher place.

G-D GIVES US CHALLENGES TO LIFT US UP.

JUST AS BETZALEL DID WHEN MAKING THE MISHKAN. ◎

We use the world as we find it now and transform it into the Holy of Holies.

Holy Sparks

RABBI MOSHE MILLER
SHIFRA CHANA HENDRIE

Global Geula Summit

WWW.HOLYSPARKS.COM
©2020 Rae Shagalov

"CONVERSATIONS FROM THE EDGE OF HUMAN POTENTIAL"

"THE SPIRITUAL STRUCTURE OF THE UNIVERSE: EXPANDING THE RELATIONSHIP BETWEEN MAN, GOD & WORLD"

בס"ד

SOUL ADVENTURE #24

Make a list of words of emunah to say during
challenging times to help you strengthen your faith.

ב"ה

Geulah
is about each
of us revealing
our hidden light
and bringing it
into the world.
NOTHING IN TORAH IS JUST
CONCEPTUAL BECAUSE TORAH
IS DIVINE LIGHT.
IT CHANGES US.

Emunah is
a soul power,
supernal knowing.

NOT-KNOWING AND DOING IT
ANYWAY, TRUSTING WHAT
WE KNOW, EVEN WHEN WE
DON'T KNOW WHY WE KNOW IT.

Emunah is trust in G-d
that's based on
our higher knowledge.

Action
activates
emunah.

It's a quantum leap
into greatness.

ORIT ESTHER RITER
SHIFRA CHANA HENDRIE

Global Geula Summit

G-d
wants
us to
heal.

THAT'S WHY THERE
ARE SO MANY WONDERFUL
TYPES OF THERAPIES.

Torah
is learning
and integrating
the G-dly light
into our own
being.

TORAH IS
BEYOND OUR KNOWING,
SO WE CONNECT THROUGH
ACTION @ MITZVAHS AND
KINDNESS.

G-D HAS HIS
OWN DIVINE
CALCULATIONS,
WHEN AND HOW
LONG A PERSON
NEEDS TO GO
THROUGH
HARDSHIPS,
UNTIL THEY'VE
ACQUIRED THE
GROWTH THAT
THEY NEED
THROUGH
THAT PROCESS.
THEN THE
REDEMPTION
COMES IN ITS
OWN UNIQUE
WAY.

SPEAK WORDS OF
EMUNA, "I'M HAVING
A REALLY TOUGH DAY TODAY,
BUT I KNOW G-D IS
TAKING CARE OF ME. I FEEL
G-D'S WARM EMBRACE.
I'M JUST WAITING FOR IT
TO BECOME REVEALED."
WE SPEAK TO STIMULATE OUR
SOUL POWER OF EMUNAH,
TO ALLOW OUR CROWN TO OPEN
UP TO RECEIVE THAT LIGHT OF
UNDERSTANDING, FROM THAT
WHICH WE SPOKE.

Holy Sparks

"CLEARING THE PATH TO BEING YOU"

בס"ד

SOUL ADVENTURE #25

What do you need to heal in your life?
What healing tools can you use to help you heal it?

Holy Sparks
WWW.HOLYSPARKS.COM
© 2020 Rae Shagalov

ב"ה

Everything that G‑d does is for the very best.

PUSH YOUR EMUNAH BUTTON!

G‑d will never give us a broken existence without tools to be able to correct it.

It's time to clear it out. It's time to let it go.

THIS IS THE LAST GENERATION OF GALUS, AND THE FIRST GENERATION OF GEULAH. WE STILL HAVE A LITTLE BIT OF GALUS IN US. IT'S TIME TO CLEAR IT AND FIX IT.

You have the light inside of you.

G‑D WILL NOT GIVE US ANY EXPERIENCE THAT WE CAN'T HANDLE, BECAUSE AS HE GIVES US THE EXPERIENCE AND THE CHALLENGE, HE GIVES US A BEAUTIFUL TOOLBOX WITH THE BEST TOOLS WE NEED TO REBUILD OUR LIVES. AS WE GET THE DIFFICULTY, WE ALSO GET THE SOLUTION.

WE ARE BUILDING AND REBUILDING WHAT OUR ANCESTORS HAVE LEFT UNDONE SO THAT WE CAN HEAL FROM ALL THAT LIMITS US FROM ATTACHING TO THE GOODNESS OF G‑D.

G‑d is fair.

It's not just your own redemption. Your struggle to overcome your challenges fixes all of the generations.

G‑d's goal is to bring the Redemption. He wants us to heal.

You have the healing inside of you.

ORIT ESTHER RITER
SHIFRA CHANA HENDRIE

Global Geula Summit

"CONVERSATIONS FROM THE EDGE OF HUMAN POTENTIAL"

Holy Sparks
www.HOLYSPARKS.COM
©2020 Rae Shagalov

"CLEARING THE PATH TO BEING YOU"

SOUL ADVENTURE #26

What is holding you back?
What are some possible ways
that it could heal you and set you free?

The things that hold us back ב"ה
are meant to free us from our
limitations and heal us.

We are
doing
the work.
We don't
yet see
the results
results
of the
cosmic
process,
but we
have to
have
emunah to
understand
that bigger
things are
Happening.

G‑d is
with us,
hidden
in the
pain

G‑d's plan
does not
have to be
from a place
of suffering.

But pain
is a part
of the
process.

We are all making great
leap steps in Redemption
through our efforts.

When we discover G‑d in the pain,
the Fatherly love of G‑d,
that in itself is the healing.

ORIT ESTHER RITER
SHIFRA CHANA HENDRIE

Holy
Sparks

WWW.HOLYSPARKS.COM
©2020 Rae Shagalov

Global Geula Summit   "CLEARING THE PATH TO BEING YOU"
"CONVERSATIONS FROM THE EDGE OF HUMAN POTENTIAL"

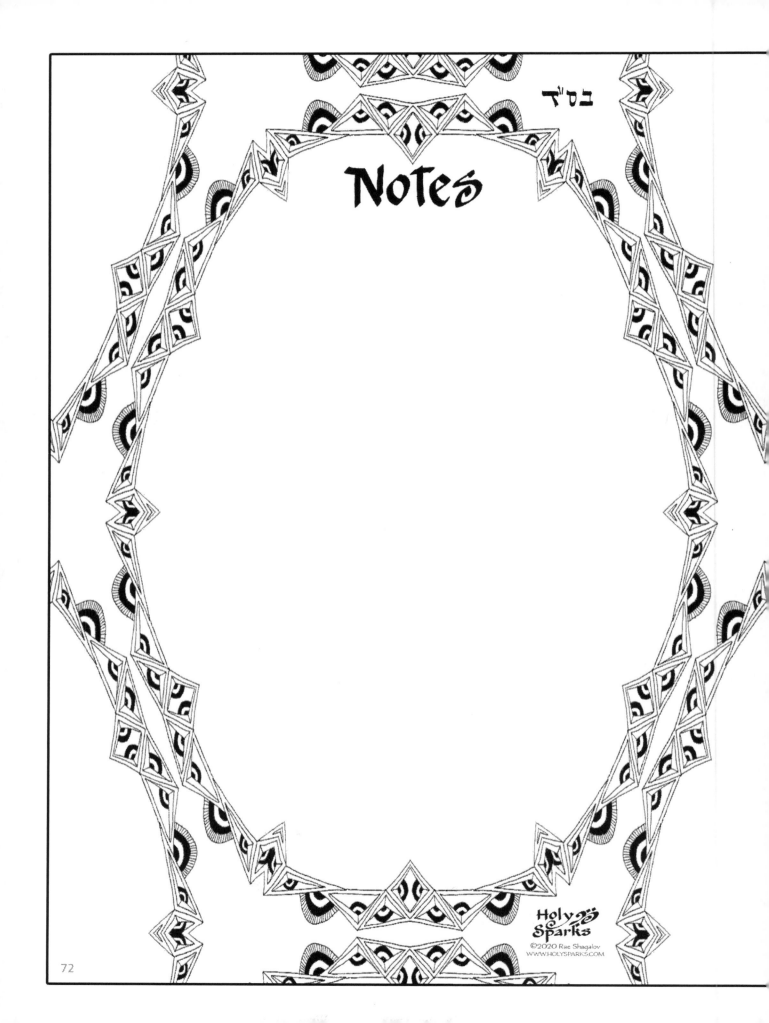

Notes

בס"ד

We're all one big cholent pot. We're all in this together.

When I heal myself, I am healing you because we are all connected.

You're the potato and I'm the bean. We're tossed into the pot of this world together, raw, in a confused mess. Then G-d turns on the heat under us. We boil, and roil, and simmer until the Shabbos of Creation, when all of our pain and struggles and triumphs will transform into a tasty cholent. Of Geulah.

Orit Esther Riter
Shifra Chana Hendrie   "Clearing the Path to Being You"

Global Geula Summit
"Conversations from the Edge of Human Potential"

Holy Sparks
www.holysparks.com
©2020 Rae Shagalov

73

SOUL ADVENTURE #27

How do you want to grow and change?

The spark of Divine Light is infinite, everywhere, at all times, simultaneously.

ב"ה

To be with G-d, you have to be like G-d.

YOU HAVE TO BE WILLING TO REFINE YOURSELF. SPIRITUAL REFINEMENT TAKES WORK. YOU HAVE TO GO DEEP AND MAKE IT ALWAYS NEW.

5 Levels of the Soul

The Soul is a piece of G-d.

1. **Yechida** SUBLIMELY UNITED WITH G-D.

2. **Chaya** NULLIFICATION OF THE EGO IN THE TRANSCENDENT ABSOLUTE TRUTH OF G-D.

3. **Neshama** G-D BREATHES FROM HIS INNERMOST SELF INTO THE SOUL.

4. **Ruach** THE INTELLECT CONTEMPLATES AND AROUSES THE EMOTIONS TO LOVE AND FEAR OF G-D.

5. **Nefesh** LOWEST LEVEL OF THE SOUL WHERE IT RESTS IN THE BODY AND PROVIDES THE LIFE FORCE.

EVERYTHING WE DO AFFECTS A DIFFERENT PART OF THE SOUL.

It all starts with the will and desire to grow & change.

As you rectify yourself, you also rectify the world.

THE WORLD AT ITS CORE HAS INFINITE LIGHT WHICH MEANS IT CAN BE ANYTHING.

Torah teaches the path of perfection.

Infinite possibilities exist at all times!

"CREATING A RECTIFIED, DIVINE WORLD"
RABBI PINCHAS WINSTON
SHIFRA CHANA HENDRIE
Global Geula Summit
"CONVERSATIONS FROM THE EDGE OF HUMAN POTENTIAL"

Holy Sparks
WWW.HOLYSPARKS.COM
©2020 Rae Shagalov

בס"ד

SOUL ADVENTURE #28
WHO ARE YOU AT THE CORE?
Set a timer for 5 minutes. Ask yourself, "Who am I?"
Write down your answer. Repeat until the timer signals to stop.

The greatest pleasure in life is being connected to G-d.

HOW? BY BEING FULLY WHO YOU TRULY ARE IN YOUR ESSENCE.

THE MORE WE REVEAL G-DLINESS IN THIS WORLD THROUGH TORAH AND MITZVAHS, THE LESS WE'LL FEEL A JOLT WHEN MOSHIACH COMES.

IF WHAT YOU ARE LEARNING IS NOT CHANGING YOU AND MAKING YOU MORE G-DLY, YOU'RE NOT REALLY LEARNING IT.

We are entering a time of miraculous awakening.

YOU HAVE TO TRAIN YOUR FORMER SELF FOR A NEW, DIFFERENT, HIGHER LEVEL OF SELF.

Go deeper, and deeper, and deeper until you get to the core.

REACH TO THE HIGHER LEVELS OF YOUR SOUL.

EXILE Galus IT'S BAD AND WE'VE GOT TO FIX IT.

vs.

Geulah IT'S WONDERFUL AND WE HAVE TO REVEAL IT. WE ARE MEANT TO TAKE THIS JOURNEY WHICH IS THE COMPLETENESS OF MAN WHICH IS THE COMPLETENESS OF G-D'S PLAN.

Connect to G-d in prayer until you are beyond eyverything.

G-D DOESN'T RECYCLE SOULS BECAUSE HE RAN OUT OF THEM; G-D SENDS OUR SOULS DOWN FOR SPECIFIC RECTIFICATIONS. WE ARE MEANT TO GROW TO COMPLETION.

All good is G-d.

Every bit of good you do lasts forever.

MATERIAL PLEASURES DON'T MAKE UP FOR THE LACK OF INNER JOY.

The greatest pleasure is earned through effort.

THE ULTIMATE FREEDOM AND PLEASURE IS CONTINUOUS, ACCELERATING REVELATION OF THE TRUTH OF THE DEEPER REALITY.

Holy Sparks

"CREATING A RECTIFIED, DIVINE WORLD"
RABBI PINCHAS WINSTON
SHIFRA CHANA HENDRIE

Global Geula Summit

"CONVERSATIONS FROM THE EDGE OF HUMAN POTENTIAL"

WWW.HOLYSPARKS.COM ©2020 Rae Shagalov

SOUL ADVENTURE #27

ב"ה

How can you light up the world today?

Lighting Shabbos candles is the mission statement of Jewish women:

"We are here to light up the world."

THE LUBAVITCHER REBBE REVOLUTIONIZED THE ROLE OF THE JEWISH WOMAN. HE SAID THAT WOMEN ALSO HAVE THE OBLIGATION TO LEARN TORAH AND ESPECIALLY CHASSIDUS, EVEN MORE THAN MEN. SHE NEEDS TO BE LEARNED ENOUGH TO ANSWER THE QUESTIONS OF HER CHILDREN. WOMEN HAVE A GREATER INTUITION AND WISDOM FOR LEARNING KABBALAH AND CHASSIDUS. WOMEN HAVE THE RESPONSIBILITY OF BEING THE FOUNDATION OF THE HOME AND THE INSPIRATION FOR HER HUSBAND AND CHILDREN, TO LIVE A G-D FEARING LIFE.

Every time you do a mitzvah, another good deed, you are bringing new light into the world, and making the world a better place.

Jewish women are at the forefront of Judaism, always initiating good things. JEWISH WOMEN ARE THE LEADERS OF OUR GENERATION.

You have tremendous energy and power from Paradise, from the soul work you've done before, to strengthen you in this new challenge.

RABBI AARON RASKIN
SHIFRA CHANA HENDRIE

The advantage of knowing you were reincarnated: WHEN YOU HAVE A CHALLENGE IN LIFE, YOU CAN OVERCOME THAT CHALLENGE BECAUSE YOU ARE NOT ALONE. ALL OF THE MITZVAHS AND GOOD DEEDS THAT YOUR SOUL DID IN ALL OF THE LIVES THAT YOU CAME DOWN INTO THIS WORLD, ACCOMPANY YOU AND ASSIST YOU WITH THIS NEW TASK.

"FROM ANCIENT EGYPT TO TODAY: WOMEN, REDEMPTION, & SECRETS OF THE MESSIANIC AGE"

Global Geula Summit
"CONVERSATIONS FROM THE EDGE OF HUMAN POTENTIAL"

Holy Sparks

WWW.HOLYSPARKS.COM
©2020 Rae Shagalov

SOUL ADVENTURE #28

ASK YOURSELF:

◆ What do I need to do to repair the world?
◆ What do I need to do to fix myself?
◆ What do I need to do to uplift my family?

This is the last generation of exile, and the first generation of redemption.

◆ What do I need to do to repair the world?

◆ What do I need to do to fix myself?

◆ What do I need to do to uplift my family?

◆ What is easy for you to do that makes people happy and adds light to the world? Do that.

◆ What is hardest for you to do? Do that, too.

Anything you do can change the world and bring Moshiach in this moment.

Not sure what you're here to do? Find a mentor you can connect to.

Rabbi Aaron Raskin
Shifra Chana Hendrie
"From Ancient Egypt to Today: Women, Redemption, & Secrets of the Messianic Age"

בס״ד

The Jewish women of our generation are reincarnated from the souls that left the land of Egypt. The souls of the women entered into the land of Israel but the men did not enter the land. 600,000 men died over the 40 years in the desert.

These souls have now returned.

The women have returned to bring the men back into the land of Israel, **into the ultimate Geulah** ◆

Our sages tell us that "in the merit of the righteous women, our ancestors were redeemed from Egypt." So, too, in our generation, in the merit of the righteous women, the world will be redeemed.

Women have a soul core experience of successful redemption.

No one came into this world as a mistake.

You are here in this world because G-d wants you here.

WHY AM I HERE?

What is my mission? What am I capable of doing?

Choose a mitzvah and do it.

Holy Sparks

www.holysparks.com
©2020 Rae Shagalov

Global Geula Summit

"Conversations from the Edge of Human Potential"

SOUL ADVENTURE #29
Prayer Notes

בס״ד

בס"ד

If you're not crying out to G‑d when you're praying, you're not praying.

THE BAAL SHEM TOV

Every time we pray, G‑d kisses us on the lips.

• PSALMS
• TORAH
• PRAYER

Every word of Torah and prayer we say vitalizes all of the worlds.

You cannot bother G‑d too much. G‑d loves you and wants to hear from you all the time, so keep being a noodge.

The angels are begging us — say another Psalm! Say more words of prayer!

OUR PRAYERS HAVE A GREAT EFFECT — EVERY SINGLE PRAYER!

WHEN MOSHIACH COMES, EVERY MOMENT WE ARE GOING TO EXPERIENCE A GREATER REVELATION OF G‑D'S REALITY. EVERY MOMENT WILL BE A NEW EXPERIENCE. EVERY MOMENT, WE'LL CLIMB TO A NEW LEVEL. BECAUSE G‑D IS INFINITE, THE EXPERIENCES WILL BE INFINITELY GREATER AND ETERNAL. EVERY MOMENT, WE WILL ENJOY GOING HIGHER AND HIGHER. CHASSIDUS GIVES US A TASTE OF THIS INFINITE TORAH. THIS IS THE WINE OF MOSHIACH. ON SHABBOS, THE FISH WE EAT IS THE LEVYATON, THE GREAT FISH OF GEULAH. THE KIDDUSH WINE IS THE SECRETS OF THE TORAH. THE MEAT IS TRANSFORMING THE PHYSICAL AND MAKING IT SPIRITUAL. ON SHABBOS, THIS IS HOW WE GET A LITTLE TASTE OF HOW IT WILL BE WHEN MOSHIACH COMES, AND THIS TASTE SHOULD INSPIRE US TO DO THE WORK WE NEED TO DO TO TRANSFORM THIS WORLD INTO THIS INFINITE REALITY OF GEULAH.

Every mitzvah we do today is like a seed we plant in the ground. When Moshiach comes, we will eat the fruits of the mitzvahs we do in this world.

Every single person can make a difference. "I cannot do it," is FAKE NEWS.

Holy Sparks
WWW.HOLYSPARKS.COM
©2020 Rae Shagalov

RABBI AARON RASKIN
SHIFRA CHANA HENDRIE
"FROM ANCIENT EGYPT TO TODAY: WOMEN, REDEMPTION, & SECRETS OF THE MESSIANIC AGE"

Global Geula Summit
"CONVERSATIONS FROM THE EDGE OF HUMAN POTENTIAL"

Make a map to Geulah ☺
Moshiach Action Plan

SOUL ADVENTURE #30
Make your M.A.P.

1. What talent or skill do you enjoy using?

2. What do you LOVE to do?

3. What kind of people do you enjoy being around? [family, older folks, children, special needs, etc.]

4. What are the problems, needs & wants of the kinds of people you enjoy?

5. What product or service could you happily create or offer with your talents, interests, strengths, or skills to help that person or group of people solve their problems or fill their lack?

6. What is one small action step you could take to get this started?

7. What is the soonest you could do this & who could help you?

Bring Moshiach with your Talents Today!

It starts with the women.

we each have 2 Moshiachs inside of us.

PUSHING AWAY EVIL AND ADDING TO GOOD DEEDS.

Every day, we have to fight the war of G-d.

Moshiach Ben Yosef

OX

WARRIOR, WILL FIGHT THE WARS OF G-D. BRINGS THE WORLD TO PURITY AND HOLINESS. REMOVES THE IDOLS OF THE WORLD. UNIFIES THE WORLD. MOSHIACH BEN YOSEF WILL DIE, AS HIS SPIRITUAL PURPOSE WILL END, AS EVIL IS BANISHED FROM THE WORLD. AMALEK REPRESENTS DOUBT, LACK OF ENTHUSIASM. MOSHIACH BEN YOSEF WILL DEFEAT AMALEK.

Moshiach Ben David.

DONKEY

TEACHER, CARRIES THE BOOKS OF TORAH, WILL REVEAL THE NEW SECRETS TO THE WORLD. HUMBLE. GIVES CHARITY, PRAYS, LEARNS TORAH.

Both Moshiachs are in every generation, preparing the world for Geulah.

Moshiach could come this moment.

WE have to bring Moshiach TODAY!

MOSHIACH IS LATE. ALL OF THE DATES HAVE PASSED. WE HAVE ALREADY COMPLETED THE WORK. MOSHIACH HAS TO COME THIS SECOND.

THE LUBAVITCHER REBBE TEACHES US TO FOCUS ON MOSHIACH COMING TODAY. ELIYAHU THE PROPHET DOES NOT HAVE TO COME FIRST. THE WAR OF GOG AND MAGOG HOPEFULLY WILL NEVER HAPPEN, BUT IF IT HAS TO HAPPEN, IT ALREADY HAPPENED IN THE WORLD WARS.

we have to receive Moshiach within our self.

EACH PERSON — YOU KNOW IN YOUR HEART WHAT YOU MUST DO TO BRING MOSHIACH. WE HAVE TO LIVE AS IF MOSHIACH IS ALREADY HERE. WE HAVE TO FEEL READY TO RECEIVE MOSHIACH THIS SECOND.

Just keep increasing your acts of goodness and kindness. Learn about Moshiach & Geulah.

RABBI AARON RASKIN
SHIFRA CHANA HENDRIE
"FROM ANCIENT EGYPT TO TODAY: WOMEN, REDEMPTION, & SECRETS OF THE MESSIANIC AGE"

Holy Sparks

Global Geula Summit
WWW.HOLYSPARKS.COM
©2020 Rae Shagalov
"CONVERSATIONS FROM THE EDGE OF HUMAN POTENTIAL"

SOUL ADVENTURE #31

Continue your Moshiach Action Plan in more detail here.

בס"ד

If I had to do just one more thing, before Moshiach could come, what would that one thing be? DO THAT!

When we all live with this excitement and integrity, Moshiach will be here.

DON'T GET BOGGED DOWN WITH DOUBTS AND DETAILS, POLITICS AND WORRIES. JUST DO MORE GOOD DEEDS, LARGE AND SMALL. INFLUENCE OTHERS TO DO SO, TOO.

What good deeds should you do? Whatever good deed you can do, do that!

The world is in a messianic state. Everyone wants a better world. Look inside yourself. You KNOW what you have to do.

The war is with our self, right now, every day. Wherever there is darkness in your life or in the world, look for the light. CONQUER YOURSELF WITH MERCY. Turn on the light in your life.

RABBI AARON RASKIN
SHIFRA CHANA HENDRIE
"FROM ANCIENT EGYPT TO TODAY: WOMEN, REDEMPTION, & SECRETS OF THE MESSIANIC AGE"

Global Geula Summit
"CONVERSATIONS FROM THE EDGE OF HUMAN POTENTIAL"

Holy Sparks
WWW.HOLYSPARKS.COM
©2020 Rae Shagalov

Notes

בס"ד

When the Torah was given, G*dliness started to become invested in the world.

THE WORLD IS RISING CONSTANTLY TO A HIGHER SPIRITUAL LEVEL. THE DIVINE ENERGY AND LIFE FORCE THAT COMES DOWN INTO THE WORLD DOESN'T HAVE SO FAR TO TRAVEL SINCE THE WORLD IS BEING LIFTED UP BIT-BY-BIT AND STAGE-BY-STAGE. THIS IS WHY TIME SEEMS SO MUCH SHORTER THAN IT USED TO BE. THE MOMENTS ARE SHORTER.

In the Messianic Era time speeds up.

In the time of Redemption physicality & spirituality merge. Then time will stop.

INSTEAD OF TIME, WE WILL EXPERIENCE PULSES OF G-DLINESS.

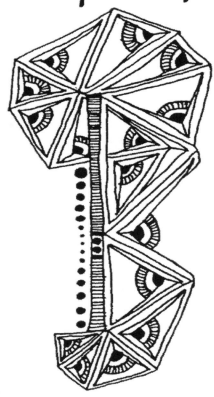

G*d did not create a perfect world. G*d created a world to be perfected by us.

RABBI AARON RASKIN
SHIFRA CHANA HENDRIE
"FROM ANCIENT EGYPT TO TODAY: WOMEN, REDEMPTION, & SECRETS OF THE MESSIANIC AGE"

Global Geula Summit

Holy Sparks

WWW.HOLYSPARKS.COM
©2020 Rae Shagalov

"CONVERSATIONS FROM THE EDGE OF HUMAN POTENTIAL"

בס"ד

SOUL ADVENTURE #32

Make a Prayer List.

Dare to dream BIG!

Transformation
TAKES DARKNESS, THE THINGS THAT GET IN OUR WAY, AND BRINGS OUT THE INNER LIGHT AND PURPOSE SO THAT THE CHALLENGE BECOMES AN OPPORTUNITY TO SHINE AND GROW.

WHEN WE PRAY FOR ANOTHER, WE STEP OUT OF OURSELVES AND INTO G-D'S PLAN.

We step into the web of connectedness that is the truth.

WHEN WE PRAY FOR ANOTHER, WE ARE ELEVATED TOGETHER WITH THEM IN HASHEM'S BIG PLAN.

Boost each other up and keep boosting, until the whole world wins!

SOMETIMES HELPING SOMEONE MEANS DO NOTHING BUT STILL PRAY.

How fast can we all start to thrive?

There are always disruptions but we can still thrive.

SOMETIMES THE DISRUPTIONS CAUSE US TO MELT DOWN, TO DISINTEGRATE, IN ORDER TO BECOME SOMETHING NEW, SOMETHING BETTER, STRONGER.

The Almighty is crazy about us,

believes in us, and knows something about us that we don't know.

"THE CREATOR'S UNCONDITIONAL LOVE"   RIVKA MALKA PERLMAN
SHIFRA CHANA HENDRIE

Global Geula Summit

"CONVERSATIONS FROM THE EDGE OF HUMAN POTENTIAL"

Holy Sparks

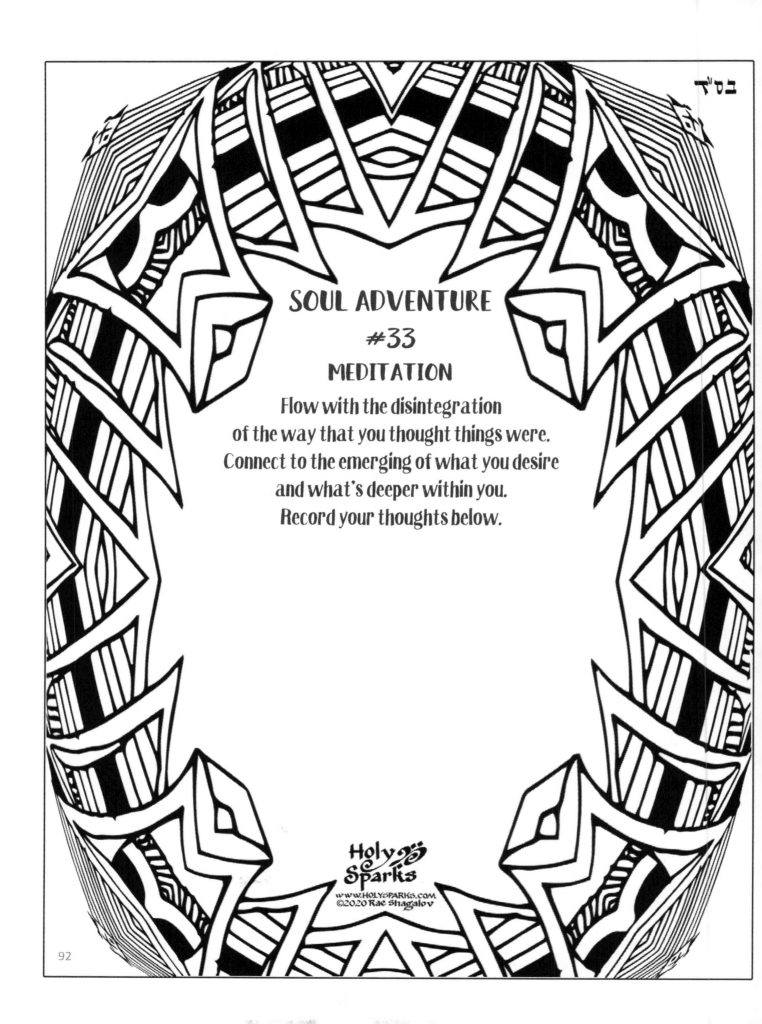

בס"ד

SOUL ADVENTURE
#33
MEDITATION

Flow with the disintegration
of the way that you thought things were.
Connect to the emerging of what you desire
and what's deeper within you.
Record your thoughts below.

ב"ה

You are not breaking, your limits are breaking.

Flow with the disintegration of the way that you thought things were.

Connect to the emerging of what you desire and what's deeper within you.

Connect

to G◌d's purpose for you, even when you don't really know what it is.

Evil is the throne of good. EVIL WAS CREATED TO SERVE GOOD.

Evil exists to bring us to a higher good.

You can be okay

Even when you're not okay.

AS A KING OR A QUEEN, YOU CAN PARDON ANYONE IN THE WORLD. YOU CAN BESTOW FORGIVENESS. YOU CAN BLESS AND PRAY FOR PEOPLE WHO HAVE HURT YOU.

Don't face darkness with darkness. Shine your light.

RIVKA MALKA PERLMAN
SHIFRA CHANA HENDRIE
"THE CREATOR'S UNCONDITIONAL LOVE"
Global Geula Summit
"CONVERSATIONS FROM THE EDGE OF HUMAN POTENTIAL"

Holy Sparks

WWW.HOLYSPARKS.COM
©2020 Rae Shagalov

בס"ד

SOUL ADVENTURE #34

Take a moment to really appreciate
the wonderful human being that you are!
Write your good qualities below.

Holy
Sparks

בס"ד

The truth of G‑d's love for us:

G‑d loves our:

mistakes,
humanity,
fears,
innocence,
falls,
rises.

G‑d doesn't only love us when we're getting it all right.

G‑d's love for us sustains our very being.

You can't mess it up.

G‑d wants you to succeed in your personal mission AND DOES NOT PAUSE FROM OVERSEEING YOUR JOURNEY FOR EVEN ONE SECOND.

G‑d never gives up on you!

You are G‑d's favorite child. Of course, He will never give up on you. TAKE A MOMENT TO APPRECIATE THE WONDERFUL HUMAN BEING THAT YOU ARE!

"THE CREATOR'S UNCONDITIONAL LOVE"

RIVKA MALKA PERLMAN
SHIFRA CHANA HENDRIE

Holy Sparks

Global Geula Summit

"CONVERSATIONS FROM THE EDGE OF HUMAN POTENTIAL"

WWW.HOLYSPARKS.COM
©2020 Rae Shagalov

95

בס"ד

SOUL ADVENTURE #35

What dream is inside of you waiting
to come out, longing to emerge?

*The world needs this
and is waiting for you to do it!*

Holy Sparks

The ultimate purpose of Creation is to

Reveal G-d in this world.

ב"ה

G-d's presence • goodness • love •

G-D EXPRESSES HIS GOOD FOR US • THROUGH US • AS US.

Every challenge hides G-d's light. THE JOURNEY IS TO ALLOW THE PAIN AND DISCOMFORT TO LIFT YOU UP.

Whatever dream is inside of you waiting to come out

Longing to emerge

The infinite Divine Light wants to shine through YOU!

THIS IS THE WORLD OF ACTION.

Let it out!

THE WORLD NEEDS IT AND IS WAITING FOR YOU to do it.

"THE CREATOR'S UNCONDITIONAL LOVE"

RIVKA MALKA PERLMAN
SHIFRA CHANA HENDRIE

Global Geula Summit

"CONVERSATIONS FROM THE EDGE OF HUMAN POTENTIAL"

Holy Sparks

WWW.HOLYSPARKS.COM
©2020 Rae Shagalov

בס"ד

SOUL ADVENTURE #36

How can you share the light of Torah?
With whom can you share it?

Holy Sparks WWW.HOLYSPARKS.COM ©2020 Rae Shagalov

The purpose of the Jew is to shine the light of Torah to the world, and this will bring Geulah.

WHEN WE ARE DOING OUR JOB AND SHARING THE LIGHT OF TORAH, THEN THE PEOPLE OF THE WORLD CHANGE THEIR VIEW OF G-D AND SEEK TO LOVE HASHEM. WHEN THEY LOVE THE ALMIGHTY, THEY EXPRESS THEIR LOVE BY LOVING THE NATION OF ISRAEL.

G-d says, ב"ה The Land of Israel belongs to the People of Israel.

WHEN MOSHIACH COMES, ALL OF THE NATIONS OF THE WORLD WILL EMBRACE THE G-D OF ABRAHAM, ISAAC, & JACOB.

The Jewish people can never be destroyed.

The Messianic Age is now unfolding. We are seeing the splendor and the wonder of the prophecies unfolding before our eyes!

THE PURPOSE OF ANTISEMITISM IS TO GET THE JEWS BACK ON TRACK, RETURNING TO G-D & DOING MITZVAHS.

THE COMING OF MOSHIACH AND THE REDEMPTIVE PROCESS CAN ONLY HAPPEN BY THE JEWS DOING THEIR JOB.

NOW is the time to fully embrace Torah.

The core of antisemitism: The person who hates the Jew is at war with G-d.

Antisemitism is a result of a deep, profound hatred of the Almighty.

THEY HATE THE G-D OF ISRAEL. BUT HOW DO YOU GO TO WAR AGAINST THE CREATOR OF THE HEAVEN AND THE EARTH?

YOU CAN'T. SO THEY GO AFTER G-D'S FIRSTBORN SON, THE NATION OF ISRAEL.

Holy Sparks
www.HOLYSPARKS.com
©2020 Rae Shagalov

Global Geula Summit

RABBI TOVIA SINGER
SHIFRA CHANA HENDRIE
"THE WORLD WILL BE FILLED WITH THE KNOWLEDGE OF G-D" UNIVERSAL TORAH AND THE NATIONS OF THE WORLD

"CONVERSATIONS FROM THE EDGE OF HUMAN POTENTIAL"

World Peace NOW!
7 Universal Laws for All Mankind.
The Only Hope for all of humanity!

① Belief in G‑d.
Don't worship idols

② Honor G‑d.
Don't be disrespectful to G‑d with your speech.

③ Preserve Human Life.
Do not murder. Value the sanctity of all human lives.

④ Respect Family Relationships.
No acts that undermine traditional family life.

⑤ Respect other's property.
Even if times get tough, don't cheat others or steal their money or stuff.

⑥ Show compassion for animals.
Don't eat meat that came from a live animal. No cruelty to animals!

⑦ Establish Honest Courts.
Uphold a just legal system.

The Seven Laws of Noah — G‑d's Rules for All Humanity

For more info go to:
asknoah.org
holysparks.com

Holy Sparks
©2020 Rae Shagalov
WWW.HOLYSPARKS.COM

בס"ד

B'nei Noach The children of Noah,

IS A TERM USED FOR NON-JEWS WHO EMBRACE THE TENETS OF THE JEWISH FAITH BUT DO NOT JOIN THE JEWISH NATION.

Noahides

KEEP 7 CATEGORIES OF LAWS. THEY HAVE UNIQUE MITZVOT. TO OBSERVE, NOT BECAUSE IT MAKES SENSE, BUT BECAUSE THE G-D OF ISRAEL COMMANDED IT. THIS IS THE HIGHEST LEVEL OF TORAH FOR THE NON-JEW. THIS IS MESSIANIC.

Deep inside, everyone knows there is a Creator.

IN THEIR HEART OF HEARTS, EVERY PERSON KNOWS THERE IS A G-D. THEY MIGHT BE ALIENATED BY ORGANIZED RELIGION OR BY PEOPLE IN THEIR COMMUNITY, BUT ULTIMATELY, NO RATIONAL MIND CAN DENY THAT THERE IS A CREATOR OF THE UNIVERSE.

Torah is the blueprint for Creation.

Torah has a place for everybody. You don't have to become a Jew to have a place in the World-to-Come.

YOU JUST HAVE TO OBSERVE THE MITZVAHS THAT ARE APPROPRIATE FOR YOU, ACCORDING TO THE TORAH.

TORAH DESCRIBES HOW EVERYTHING WORKS ON THE DEEPEST LEVELS AND SHOWS THE PATH TO A PEACEFUL, UNIFIED, DIVINE WORLD.

Kiss Hashem with all your heart!

RABBI TOVIA SINGER
SHIFRA CHANA HENDRIE
"THE WORLD WILL BE FILLED WITH THE KNOWLEDGE OF G-D" UNIVERSAL TORAH AND THE NATIONS OF THE WORLD.

Global Geula Summit

"CONVERSATIONS FROM THE EDGE OF HUMAN POTENTIAL"

SOUL ADVENTURE #37

What is one small good change
you could begin to make today?

Teshuva
IS THE RETURN
TO THE ESSENTIAL
SELF. IT DOESN'T
JUST MEAN TAKING
ON A NEW RESOLUTION.
IT ALSO MEANS DOING
SOMETHING THAT YOU
ARE ALREADY DOING,
AND DOING IT EVEN
BETTER IN A SPECIAL WAY.

בס"ד

בס"ד

What if you do something you regret?

Sin is not a person, it's an event.

That event happened yesterday. Yesterday ended last night.

Sin does NOT define who you are.

Today is a new day.

If you return to G-d's ways, you will be forgiven completely.

You are created in G-d's image.

G-D IS NOT CREATED IN MAN'S IMAGE. YOU MIGHT THINK A CERTAIN PERSON WILL NEVER FORGIVE YOU, BUT THAT IS NOT TRUE FOR G-D.

THE LAND OF ISRAEL IS ONLY COMPATIBLE WITH THE JEWISH PEOPLE BECAUSE G-D GAVE THE LAND OF ISRAEL TO THE JEWS. THERE IS NO GREATER SIGN OF THE IMPENDING REDEMPTION THAN THE RETURN OF THE JEWS TO THEIR LAND AND THAT THE LAND GIVES FORTH ITS PRODUCE. IF YOU WANT A SIGN THAT REDEMPTION IS HERE, GO TO THE SHUK IN JERUSALEM. THROUGHOUT OUR EXILE THE LAND OF ISRAEL WAS BARREN, IT WON'T PRODUCE FOR ANYONE BUT THE CHILDREN OF ISRAEL.

It's time to come home

IT IS THE REPENTANCE OF THE JEWS THAT TRIGGERS THE MESSIANIC AGE. ISAIAH 59

May we merit to witness the coming of the true Moshiach speedily in our time.

Holy Sparks

www.holysparks.com
©2020 Rae Shagalov

Global Geula Summit

RABBI TOVIA SINGER
SHIFRA CHANA HENDRIE
"THE WORLD WILL BE FILLED WITH THE KNOWLEDGE OF G-D" UNIVERSAL TORAH AND THE NATIONS OF THE WORLD

"CONVERSATIONS FROM THE EDGE OF HUMAN POTENTIAL"

103

בס"ד

SOUL ADVENTURE #38

What is one mitzvah you could do or improve to light up the world?

We are in this together.

This world is a place of tremendous darkness.

When you do a mitzvah you light up the world.

After thousands of years of exile and persecution, many Jews are lost and weary.

When Jews see that non-Jews are looking for Torah with open hearts, it opens our hearts, too.

We see the fulfillment of prophecy through you and that arouses us to return to G*d, and to our mission, and our destiny to be a light unto the nations.

Holy Sparks

WWW.HOLYSPARKS.COM
©2020 Rae Shagalov

Global Geula Summit

RABBI TOVIA SINGER
SHIFRA CHANA HENDRIE
"THE WORLD WILL BE FILLED WITH THE KNOWLEDGE OF G-D" UNIVERSAL TORAH AND THE NATIONS OF THE WORLD

"CONVERSATIONS FROM THE EDGE OF HUMAN POTENTIAL"

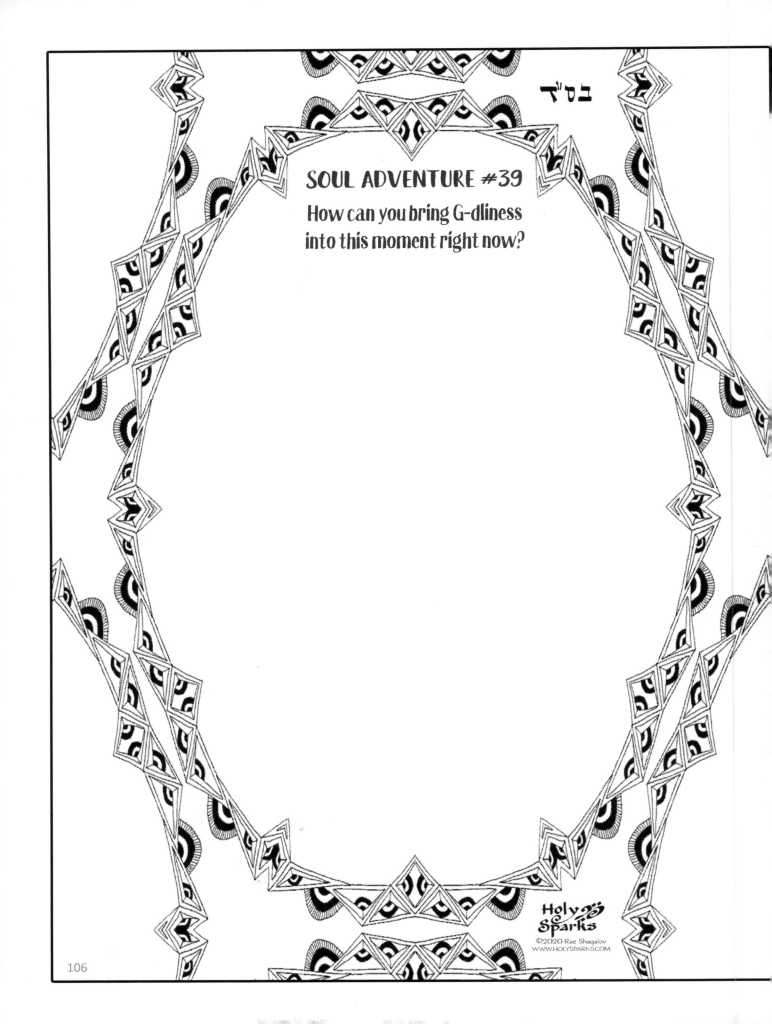

בס"ד

SOUL ADVENTURE #39

How can you bring G-dliness
into this moment right now?

In every moment is the past, present, and future, all at the same time.

When we bring G·dliness into this moment, we bring the Geulah of the future, into the present.

THE WORLD-TO-COME IS THE ULTIMATE STATE OF THE WORLD AFTER THE MESSIANIC PROCESS IS COMPLETE, AT THE END OF THE 7TH MILLENIUM.

To reach the top of the ladder, it has to be entrenched in the earth.

THE JEWISH PATH DOES NOT DENY THE PHYSICAL, IT EMBRACES THE PHYSICAL AND TRANSFORMS AND ELEVATES IT INTO THE SPIRITUAL. JEWS ARE BORN TO EXPRESS OUR SPIRITUALITY BY FIXING AND HEALING THE WORLD.

The ultimate redemptive energy is not to escape this world, but to uplift and purify it.

Obstacles into opportunities, Trials into triumphs... why is there so much struggle in this world?

WE ARE MEANT TO EARN OUR PORTION OF THE WORLD-TO-COME SO THAT WE WON'T "EAT THE BREAD OF SHAME." LEARNING THE INNER DIMENSIONS OF THE TORAH HELPS US OVERCOME OUR CHALLENGES WITH JOY.

All that G·d expects of each of us is to do our own little part in our own little corner of the universe.

The Jewish people are a nation of leaders.

WHEN ENOUGH PEOPLE HAVE ACTIVATED THEIR PERSONAL SPARK OF MOSHIACH, IT WILL CREATE A CRITICAL MASS OF ENERGY THAT WILL BRING THE MESSIANIC ERA.

RABBI AVRAHAM ARIEH TRUGMAN
SHIFRA CHANA HENDRIE   "ACCESSING DIVINITY AND GEULAH"

Global Geula Summit

"CONVERSATIONS FROM THE EDGE OF HUMAN POTENTIAL"

Holy Sparks

WWW.HOLYSPARKS.COM
©2020 Rae Shagalov

בס"ד

SOUL ADVENTURE #40

How can you activate your own personal spark of Moshiach?

We are here to bring Geulah. We are meant to do our part to stimulate G‑d to do His part. MOSHIACH IS COMING FOR ALL PEOPLE. ALL WE CAN DO IS WHAT WE CAN DO IN OUR OWN LITTLE WORLD BY BEING KIND, LOVING & RESPECTFUL TO THOSE AROUND US.

WE HAVE A SOUL AND A RELATIONSHIP WITH G‑D. ELEVATE AND ACTIVATE YOUR SOUL AND FIX WHAT YOU CAN FIX AROUND YOU.

PEOPLE GO THROUGH VERY HARD THINGS. IF ALL WE CAN SEE AND FEEL IS THE PAIN, WE LOSE HOPE. BUT, BECAUSE WE CAN SEE THE FUTURE IN THE PRESENT, WE CAN KNOW AND TRUST IT WILL BE GOOD.

We each have a spark of Moshiach inside of us.

When we activate this spark, we bring Geulah from the future world into the present.

The Jewish people are compared to an olive tree. Why?

TO GET THE OIL, YOU HAVE TO CRUSH THE OLIVES. THE MORE YOU CRUSH THE OLIVES, THE MORE OIL IS EXTRACTED. THIS IS LIKE THE JEWISH PEOPLE. THE MORE WE WERE OPPRESSED AND CHALLENGED IN EXILE, THE MORE HOLINESS WE PRODUCED. THIS IS HOW THE TALMUD DESCRIBED THE PURPOSE OF PAIN IN THE EXILE.

Moshiach will cause a revolution in consciousness.

The Goal is to bring the Torah to all people.

THE SPIRITUALITY YOU ARE SEARCHING FOR IS IN YOUR OWN JEWISH BACKYARD. LOOK FOR THE DEEP, INNER WISDOM OF TORAH.

OUR MISSION IS TO BRING THE ONE G‑D TO ALL NATIONS, TO UNITE THE WHOLE WORLD.

RABBI AVRAHAM ARIEH TRUGMAN
SHIFRA CHANA HENDRIE

"ACCESSING DIVINITY AND GEULAH"

Global Geula Summit

"CONVERSATIONS FROM THE EDGE OF HUMAN POTENTIAL"

Holy Sparks

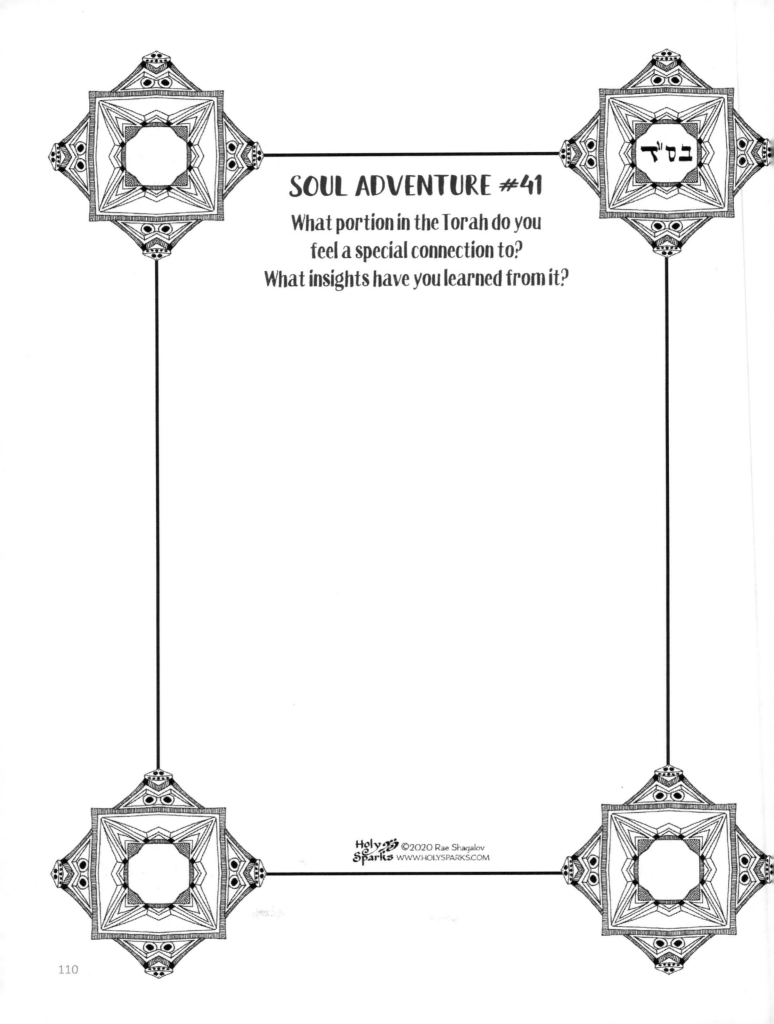

SOUL ADVENTURE #41

What portion in the Torah do you
feel a special connection to?
What insights have you learned from it?

ב״ד

The 10 Sefirot are the kabbalistic map of reality.

THEY ARE 10 CHANNELS OF DIVINE FLOW AND EXPRESSION INTO CREATION. THE 10 SEFIROT AND 22 PATHWAYS CONNECT THE PHYSICAL AND SPIRITUAL REALMS. EVERY SOUL IN THE UNIVERSE IS CONNECTED TO ONE OF THESE SEFIROT, AT THE ROOT OF THE SOUL.

As below, so above.

THE ORAL TORAH ACCORDING TO RAV TZADOK:

THE SUM TOTAL OF THE INSIGHTS PRESSED FROM THE HEARTS OF JEWS STRIVING TO LIVE THEIR LIVES IN ACCORDANCE WITH THE TRUTHS THAT THEY ABSORBED AT SINAI.

We all have a portion in the Torah. Studying Torah to know G-d is an act of devotion, love, and union.

THE GOAL OF MEDITATION IS TO ACCESS OUR PURE, UNSELF-CONSCIOUS CORE, TO DROP INTO A DEEPER LEVEL OF SOUL, TO CLEANSE OUR LENS OF PERSONALITY THAT DISTORTS REALITY.

Prayer is a powerful tool for refining the will.

A DELICATE NEGOTIATION BETWEEN THE HEAD AND THE HEART, BETWEEN THE SELF AND G-D, THE SERVICE OF THE HEART

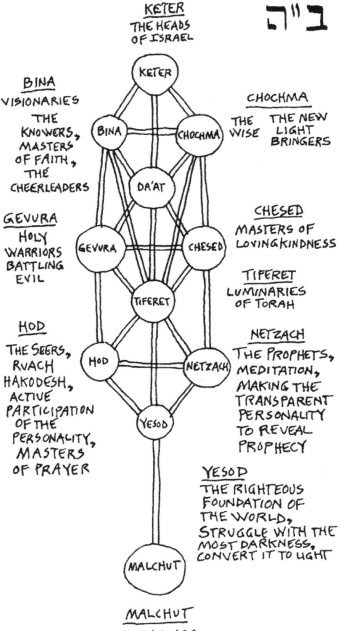

KETER
THE HEADS OF ISRAEL

בס"ד

BINA
VISIONARIES THE KNOWERS, MASTERS OF FAITH, THE CHEERLEADERS

CHOCHMA
THE WISE — THE NEW LIGHT BRINGERS

GEVURA
HOLY WARRIORS BATTLING EVIL

CHESED
MASTERS OF LOVING KINDNESS

TIFERET
LUMINARIES OF TORAH

HOD
THE SEERS, RUACH HAKODESH, ACTIVE PARTICIPATION OF THE PERSONALITY, MASTERS OF PRAYER

NETZACH
THE PROPHETS, MEDITATION, MAKING THE TRANSPARENT PERSONALITY TO REVEAL PROPHECY

YESOD
THE RIGHTEOUS FOUNDATION OF THE WORLD, STRUGGLE WITH THE MOST DARKNESS, CONVERT IT TO LIGHT

MALCHUT
THE KINGS MASTERY SELF-MASTERY SURRENDER TO OUR DEEPEST & MOST AUTHENTIC TRUTH

SARAH YEHUDIT SCHNEIDER
SHIFRA CHANA HENDRIE
"LIVING AS A PARTNER IN CREATION AND THE UNIQUE ROOT/ROLE OF YOUR SOUL"

Global Geula Summit

"CONVERSATIONS FROM THE EDGE OF HUMAN POTENTIAL"

Holy Sparks

WWW.HOLYSPARKS.COM
©2020 Rae Shagalov

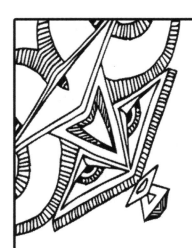

SOUL ADVENTURE #42

Ask yourself:

"what do I really want?"

Write your answer down.

Repeat this 20 times

Ask yourself:
"What do I really want?"

You are not fatally flawed.
This is where you fit.
This is your path.
These are your struggles,
and you're not the only one.
Wherever your soul is rooted,
that's where your flaw is,
and that's where your work is.

In your rectification is the rectification of the whole world.

Move yourself from supression to a deeper expression of who you truly are. This is Geulah.

GO SO DEEP INTO THE SUPPRESSION OF YOUR PASSION UNTIL YOU UNDERSTAND ITS TRUE PURPOSE.

ב"ה

Passion is your access to infinity.

BRING YOUR PASSION TO ITS ROOT OF A PASSION FOR G-DLINESS, FOR LIGHT, FOR SOUL EXPRESSION, FOR LIFE, FOR LOVE. CONNECT YOUR PASSION TO ITS SOURCE, AND TO GEULAH, THE INFINITE WORLD THAT NEVER ENDS.

EVERYTHING INFLUENCES EVERYTHING ALL OF THE TIME. EVERYTHING WE DO RADIATES THROUGHOUT THE ENTIRE UNIVERSE, AFFECTS EVERY THING, AND COMES BACK TO US.

Everything we elevate, elevates everything.

SARAH YEHUDIT SCHNEIDER
SHIFRA CHANA HENDRIE
"LIVING AS A PARTNER IN CREATION AND THE UNIQUE ROOT/ROLE OF YOUR SOUL"

Holy Sparks

Global Geula Summit
"CONVERSATIONS FROM THE EDGE OF HUMAN POTENTIAL"

WWW.HOLYSPARKS.COM
©2020 Rae Shagalov

SOUL ADVENTURE #43

Who or what in your life
disturbs your peace?
How can you elevate the Holy Spark
that is trapped in that person or situation?

בס"ד

An enemy is an upside-down soulmate.

In the breaking of the vessels...

THE UNIVERSE SHATTERED, OUR SOULS SHATTERED, THE TORAH SHATTERED, EVERYTHING SHATTERED. WE COME INTO THIS WORLD WITH ONLY PART OF OUR SOUL. THERE ARE STILL SHATTERED PIECES OF OUR SOUL SCATTERED THROUGHOUT THE WORLD. THESE ARE THE HOLY SPARKS WE MUST FIND. G-D GUIDES US, MOMENT BY MOMENT, TO WHERE WE NEED TO GO TO FIND THESE HOLY SPARKS THAT WE ARE MEANT TO RESTORE AND ELEVATE TO HOLINESS.

To raise the Holy Sparks is to reveal and restore the truth.

BUT THIS IS NOT ALWAYS DONE THROUGH THE MIND. WE KNOCK AGAINST THIS, AND SCRAPE AGAINST THAT UNTIL EVEN THE BODY REVEALS THE TRUTH.

Everything in this world has a role to play in Geulah.

WE ARE CONNECTED TO EVERYTHING AND EVERYTHING IS CONNECTED TO EVERYTHING. REDEEMING THE SPARKS MEANS SEEING THE TRUTH AND LOVE OF G-D IN EVERYTHING. A SHATTERED HOLY SPARK IS A PIECE OF OURSELF THAT WE DON'T RECOGNIZE AS OURSELF, IN SOMEONE OR SOMETHING ELSE.

SARAH YEHUDIT SCHNEIDER
SHIFRA CHANA HENDRIE
"LIVING AS A PARTNER IN CREATION AND THE UNIQUE ROOT/ROLE OF YOUR SOUL"

AN ENEMY IS ANYONE WHO DISTURBS YOUR PEACE. ONE OF YOUR HOLY SPARKS IS TRAPPED INSIDE OF THAT PERSON OR SITUATION. IT'S THERE FOR YOU TO ELEVATE.

Pray for your spiritual enemy's awakening and teshuva, just like you pray for your own.

THIS WILL EITHER MOVE YOUR ENEMY CLOSER TO G-D AND TRUTH, OR IT WILL TOUCH THE HOLY SPARK OF OURSELVES THAT IS INSIDE THE ENEMY AND EXTRACT IT. IF THAT PERSON IS TRULY SO EVIL AS TO BE UNREDEEMABLE, THEN THAT PRAYER WILL ACCELERATE THEIR DEMISE.

Hatred makes things worse. Prayer fixes everything.

IF THEY DO TESHUVA, THEY WIN, WE WIN, AND G-D WINS.

Holy Sparks
WWW.HOLYSPARKS.COM
©2020 Rae Shagalov

Global Geula Summit

"CONVERSATIONS FROM THE EDGE OF HUMAN POTENTIAL"

בס"ד

SOUL ADVENTURE
#44

BE A MIRACLE TODAY!

How can you surprise yourself by doing
something extra special to make yourself
into a vessel to receive a miracle?

The month of Nisan is the beginning of the year for miracles. NISSAN IS THE CHANNEL THROUGH WHICH ALL MIRACLES ENTER INTO THE COSMOS. ROSH CHODESH NISAN IS THE BEST TIME TO PRAY FOR A MIRACLE.

The best way to get a miracle is to be a miracle yourself.

BEING A MIRACLE MEANS NOT BEING PREDICTABLE, NOT BEING WHO YOU WERE YESTERDAY, SURPRISING YOURSELF BY DOING SOMETHING EXTRA SPECIAL TO MAKE YOURSELF INTO A VESSEL TO RECEIVE A MIRACLE. It's an internal discovery of a deeper self, purification from below, and Divine help from above.

Open yourself up to the G‑dliness that is accessible to you in Torah and mitzvahs, through kindness and connecting to each other.

בס״ד

The G‑dly spark in us can transcend everything!

Torah repairs the world and fixes it at the core. ALL G‑DLY LIGHT AND G‑D'S TRUTH IS EMBEDDED IN THE TORAH. WHEN WE LEARN TORAH TODAY, WE DON'T SEE THE DIVINITY IN IT. IT MIGHT SEEM LIKE DRY DETAILS, BUT IN TORAH LIES THE INFINITE WISDOM AND ESSENCE OF G‑D. WHEN MOSHIACH COMES WE WILL LEARN TORAH AND EXPERIENCE THE INFINITE LIGHT THAT'S IN IT.

Study Torah every night because Torah gladdens the heart. THIS IS HOW TO OVERCOME DEPRESSION.

Holy Sparks
WWW.HOLYSPARKS.COM
©2020 Rae Shagalov

RABBI REUVEN WOLF
SHIFRA CHANA HENDRIE
"GEULAH IS REAL! HEAVEN COMING DOWN TO EARTH BEFORE OUR EYES"

"CONVERSATIONS FROM THE EDGE OF HUMAN POTENTIAL"
Global Geula Summit

Holy Sparks
WWW.HOLYSPARKS.COM
©2020 Rae Shagalov

בס"ד

SOUL ADVENTURE #45

How can you unblock & channel the flow
of Infinite G-dly light into your life today?

Holy Sparks
www.HOLYSPARKS.COM
©2020 Rae Shagalov

118

choose life!

choose Goodness◆
choose G-dliness◆
choose to really live◆

Let that choice come from your very being & from your essence◆

WE ALL HAVE A SOUL, BUT ONLY A LITTLE PART OF OUR SOUL DESCENDS INTO OUR BODIES. ONLY A LITTLE RAY OF OUR SOUL DESCENDS. MOST OF OUR SOUL, WHICH IS OUR TRUE BEING, REMAINS ATTACHED TO G-D. THE SOURCE OF OUR SOUL IS OUR MAZAL WHICH DRIPS INTO OUR BODIES.

By creating silence in our life, we can hear our soul and sense the ripples of our G-dly soul on our life, as an inspiration or a Divine awakening;

CHASSIDUS, THE MYSTICAL TORAH, HELPS US UNDERSTAND THESE G-DLY DROPS THAT ARE DRIPPING FROM THE TRANSCENDENTAL PART OF OUR SOUL, AND HELPS US FEEL THE UNITY OF G-D. THEN WE BECOME AGENTS OF G-DLY LIGHT. MY LITTLE ME BECOMES A DIVINE FLOW. THIS IS HOW TO CONNECT TO YOUR HIGHER, DEEPER, TRUER, MORE G-DLY SELF. OUR SOUL, AT ITS SOURCE, IS TOTALLY ONE WITH THE INFINITE G-D.

Our choices are forever. The light we bring to the world is forever.

YOU CAN DESTROY A SOMETHING, BUT YOU CAN'T DESTROY A NOTHING. THE NOTHINGNESS PRECEDES THE SOMETHINGNESS OF CREATION. INFINITE POTENTIAL CANNOT BE DESTROYED. WHEN WE TAP INTO THE NOTHINGNESS OF OUR SOUL, WE ARE NOT FIXED OR STUCK IN OUR SELF-DEFINITIONS THAT ARE NOT REALLY WHO WE ARE.

We are conduits and expressions of the Infinite.

EACH ONE OF US HAS A CERTAIN AREA WHERE WE CHANNEL THE INFINITE LIGHT INTO OUR LIVES, OUR WORK, OUR FAMILIES, AND OUR NEIGHBORHOODS.

Each of us is a G-dly flow.

WHEN WE BECOME A BIG SOMETHING, WE BLOCK THE FLOW OF INFINITE G-DLINESS. WHEN WE PUT ASIDE OUR EGO TO SERVE G-D, WE OPEN THE CHANNEL OF INFINTY INTO OUR LIVES.

RABBI REUVEN WOLF
SHIFRA CHANA HENDRIE
"GEULAH IS REAL!
HEAVEN COMING DOWN TO EARTH BEFORE OUR EYES"

"CONVERSATIONS FROM THE EDGE OF HUMAN POTENTIAL"
Global Geula Summit

Holy Sparks

WWW.HOLYSPARKS.COM
©2020 Rae Shagalov

בס״ד

SOUL ADVENTURE #46

How can you make G-d feel
more real in your life?

Holy Sparks

©2020 Rae Shaqalov
WWW.HOLYSPARKS.COM

ב"ה

Sit back and watch the miracles all day long.

Everyone feels and senses Moshiach is close.

Open your eyes

Our job is to make G‑d real in our lives and in the world. THIS IS WHY WE PRAY — TO MAKE G‑D A REALITY. WE CAN TURN TO G‑D EVERY SECOND AND HE IS THERE FOR US, IN EVERY DETAIL OF OUR LIFE.

Geulah is here in the world already. All we need to do is open our eyes and see it. HOW DO WE SEE IT? BY STUDYING ABOUT MOSHIACH. THE MORE WE STUDY IT, THE MORE WE SEE GEULAH IN THE WORLD.

The desire for truth is sprouting in the collective soul of humanity.

DO A MITZVAH EVEN IF IT DOESN'T FEEL LIKE YOU. DON'T WORRY ABOUT WHAT'S YOU. JUST EXPRESS WHAT WANTS TO COME OUT FROM YOUR ESSENCE. DON'T WORRY IF IT DOESN'T FIT, THAT'S WHERE G‑D WANTS TO SEE YOU EXPRESSING YOUR G‑DLINESS.

Start from right from where you are. THE ESSENCE OF G‑D IS THE ESSENCE OF EXISTENCE. G‑D'S ESSENCE IS IN OUR LOWS, AS WELL AS OUR HIGHS. DARKNESS CAN GET IN THE WAY OF LIGHT, BUT NOT OF ESSENCE.

The more aware we become of Geulah, the faster and more painless the whole process is as it births into the world.

Be happy. When you are happy, G‑d is happy.

RABBI REUVEN WOLF
SHIFRA CHANA HENDRIE
"GEULAH IS REAL! HEAVEN COMING DOWN TO EARTH BEFORE OUR EYES"

"CONVERSATIONS FROM THE EDGE OF HUMAN POTENTIAL"
Global Geula Summit

Holy Sparks

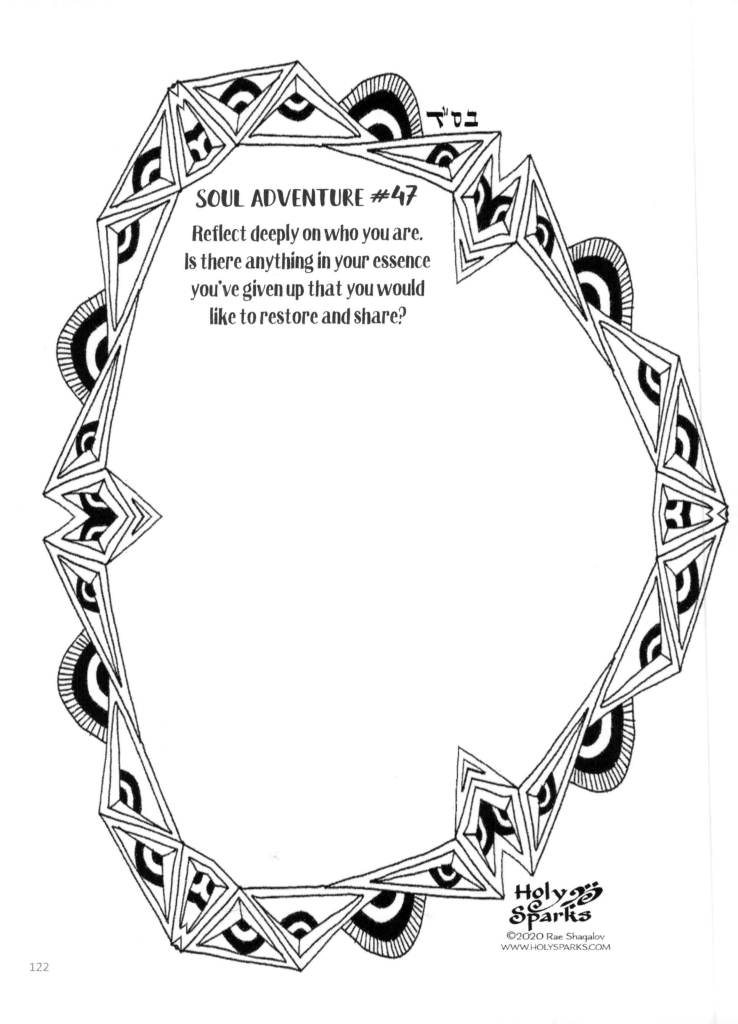

בס"ד

SOUL ADVENTURE #47

Reflect deeply on who you are.
Is there anything in your essence
you've given up that you would
like to restore and share?

בס"ד

Oneity

we are all included in the oneness of G‑d

THERE IS NO SEPARATENESS, THERE IS ONLY ONENESS IN THE PRESENCE THAT IS HERE AND NOW, AND EVERYWHERE AND ALWAYS.

This world is the ever-emerging presence of G‑d.

THROUGH PRAYER, LEARNING TORAH, AND DOING MITZVAHS, WE ARE ABLE TO ENGINEER OUR ABILITY TO BECOME MORE CONSCIOUS OF THE PRESENCE OF G-D.

In the deepest depths we are one, but not one and the same.

In love:

Lose yourself? Or find yourself?

I WANT TO FIND MYSELF IN PART OF A GREATER SELF THAT I CAN LOSE MYSELF IN. BY SURRENDERING TO A GREATER SELF, YOU BECOME EMPOWERED. EGO IS THE FALSE SELF THAT SEPARATES FROM THE GREATER SELF.

G‑d desires to be in this world.

Turn on and tune in to the channel of G‑d, to the music of shared self, the one G‑d and one soul that we are all facets of.

Love
is diversity within unity.

I'M NOT YOU AND YOU'RE NOT ME BUT WE ARE ONE. I DON'T HAVE TO GIVE UP ME FOR THERE TO BE A WE. BUT BEFORE THERE CAN BE A WE, THERE HAS TO BE A ME.

Endless Light

Move from competing to completing.

RABBI DAVID AARON
SHIFRA CHANA HENDRIE
"THE PHYSICS OF CONSCIOUSNESS & ACTIVATING DIVINE LOVE"

"CONVERSATIONS FROM THE EDGE OF HUMAN POTENTIAL"
Global Geula Summit

Holy Sparks

בס"ד

SOUL ADVENTURE #48

How can you go beyond yourself
to give love to someone who needs it?

Holy Sparks WWW.HOLYSPARKS.COM
©2020 Rae Shagalov

How to be happy ◆

Don't get stuck in yourself.

"THE MORE I CARE ABOUT ME, THE HAPPIER I'LL BE," TURNS OUT NOT TO BE TRUE.

"HOW CAN I CONTRIBUTE TO MY COMMUNITY MORE," IS THE REAL SECRET TO HAPPINESS.

Find yourself by going beyond yourself.

WE HAVE THE MITZVAH TO LOVE ALL **HUMAN BEINGS.**

LOVE HONORS BOUNDARIES.

No one is stopping you from giving love.

YOUR STRENGTHENING YOUR CONNECTION TO G-D IS WHAT ENABLES YOU TO BE A MORE COMPASSIONATE HUMAN BEING. YOUR CONNECTION TO G-D IS YOUR CONNECTION TO YOUR ROOT SELF THAT UNITES ALL HUMAN BEINGS. THE MORE YOU ARE ROOTED IN YOUR SOUL, THE MORE YOU CAN LOVE OTHERS.

To love? Or to be loved?

TO BE LOVED, YOU FEEL GOOD ABOUT YOURSELF, BUT TO LOVE, YOU FEEL EVEN BETTER. YOU FEEL MORE POWER WHEN YOU LOVE SOMEONE ELSE. YOU CAN'T FORCE SOMEONE TO LOVE YOU, BUT THAT DOESN'T STOP YOU FROM GOING OUT THERE AND LOVING. TO BE LOVED IS NOT IN YOUR CONTROL, BUT TO GIVE LOVE IS IN YOUR CONTROL.

Go do an act of kindness.

There are plenty of people in the world who could use some love, and wish someone would care ◆

ORPHANS ◆ THE ELDERLY ◆ THE HOMELESS WHO WOULD REALLY APPRECIATE A LOVING WORD, A KIND ACT, A SMILE

What's stopping you from giving love when so many people really need it?

Go forth and love!

CALL SOMEONE AND SAY, "HEY! I WAS JUST THINKING ABOUT YOU. HOW ARE YOU?" SENDING YOU MY BLESSINGS. I HOPE YOU'RE WELL."

RABBI DAVID AARON
SHIFRA CHANA HENDRIE
"THE PHYSICS OF CONSCIOUSNESS & ACTIVATING DIVINE LOVE"

" CONVERSATIONS FROM THE EDGE OF HUMAN POTENTIAL "
Global Geula Summit

Holy Sparks

בס״ד

SOUL ADVENTURE #49

Where in your day can you turn off
the noise of negativity and tune into
the channel of G-d consciousness?

The 613 commandments are the unfolding of the 10 commandments.

All of the mitzvahs are about awakening to who we are.

The mitzvahs define how we can serve to bring greater G-d consciousness to the world.

Plug in. Turn on. Tune in.

HASHEM, PLEASE USE ME. PLEASE USE ME TO BE A RECEIVER AND A TRANSMITTER OF GREATER CONSCIOUSNESS THAT WE ARE ONE AND G-D IS ONE AND WE ARE ONE WITH EACH OTHER THROUGH G-D,

Hashem! Please use me!

" IF YOU TUNE YOURSELF, THEN ONLY MUSIC WILL ENTER YOUR BEING."

Think, speak, and act in ways that align yourself with the greater self that you share with mankind.

WHAT DIFFERENCE DOES IT MAKE IF MY KNOB IS A LITTLE BIT THIS WAY OR THAT WAY? WHAT DIFFERENCE DOES IT MAKE IF THIS WIRE IS CONNECTED OR NOT CONNECTED?

TWO RADIOS HAVE A CONVERSATION. "I HAVE A SPLITTING HEADACHE. THERE'S THIS NOISE IN MY HEAD. THE OTHER RADIO SAYS, "I'M SORRY TO HEAR THAT BECAUSE I'M HEARING BEAUTIFUL MUSIC. WHAT CHANNEL ARE YOU ON?" THE OTHER RADIO SAYS, "WHAT'S A CHANNEL?"

"HEY, WE'RE RADIOS! ALL THAT NOISE IS BECAUSE YOU'RE NOT TUNED INTO THE MUSIC. THERE IS MUSIC ALL AROUND YOU, BUT IF YOU'RE NOT TUNED INTO IT, ALL YOU'LL HEAR IS NOISE."

Aloneness All Oneness

RABBI DAVID AARON
SHIFRA CHANA HENDRIE
"THE PHYSICS OF CONSCIOUSNESS & ACTIVATING DIVINE LOVE"

" CONVERSATIONS FROM THE EDGE OF HUMAN POTENTIAL "
Global Geula Summit

Holy Sparks

SOUL ADVENTURE #50

How can you build a bridge between G-d's completed vision of the world and what you're experiencing?

We are creating a bridge between ב"ה
G‑d's completed vision of the world
and what we're experiencing right now.

The ache and the invitation

to fill the gap with new light.

The 3 Phases of Creation.

① **Tohu**
CHAOS

② **Tikkun Torah**
RECTIFICATION

③ **The Era of Moshiach**
THE TRICKLING OF MESSIANIC LIGHT INTO CREATION

2000 YEARS EACH PHASE
WE ARE HERE, IN THE TRANSITION.

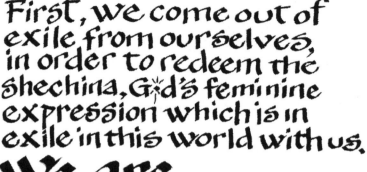

We often don't want to go to the dark but that's where the light is trapped.

First, we come out of exile from ourselves, in order to redeem the shechina, G‑d's feminine expression which is in exile in this world with us.

We are expressions of G‑d.

The entire world is shifting to the feminine expression of G‑d. The feminine aspect is the essence of the world.

WHEN WE ARE ABLE TO RECEIVE ALL OF THE LIGHT OF THE INTELLECT, ALL OF OUR FAITH IN G‑D'S ONENESS INTO THE VESSEL OF OUR HEART, THEN WE AND THE WORLD WILL BE HEALED AND WHOLE.

The way to fight darkness is through light and love.

WE IGNORE THE DARK, DON'T GET STUCK IN IT, AND LOOK FOR THE HOLY SPARK OF TRUTH AND GOODNESS THAT WANTS TO GIVE.

SOMETIMES, THE DIVINE LIGHT WE ARE RECEIVING IS SO GREAT, WE HAVE TO BE UNCONSCIOUS TO RECEIVE IT. G‑D PUT ADAM TO SLEEP SO THAT HE COULD RECEIVE THE HIGHER LIGHT OF THE FEMININE.

REBBETZIN TAMAR TABACK
SHIFRA CHANA HENDRIE
"FEMININE RISING:
WOMEN IN THE FOOTSTEPS OF MOSHIACH"

Holy Sparks
WWW.HOLYSPARKS.COM
©2020 Rae Shagalov

" CONVERSATIONS FROM THE EDGE OF HUMAN POTENTIAL "

Global Geula Summit

בס"ד

SOUL ADVENTURE #51

Where might you be out of alignment with G-d's truth?

Woman wasn't created equal to man. Woman was created with the capacity for the higher feminine consciousness

Aligning with God's truth is where the healing happens.

Levels of the Feminine

1. KLIPPAH, THE FALLEN SPARKS OF THE LIGHT THAT WAS TOO INTENSE TO BE RECEIVED— WE NEED TO DISSOLVE THIS DARKNESS BY COMING INTO OUR TRUE ESSENCE.

2. THE 2ND CHAVA WHO WOULD PREPARE THE WORLD BY REABSORBING THE LIGHT OF THE 1ST CHAVA

3. THE 3RD CHAVA, THE WOMAN WHO IS THE PERFECT BLEND OF LIGHTS AND VESSEL.

The feminine is rising in women and men.

REBBETZIN TAMAR TABACK
SHIFRA CHANA HENDRIE
"FEMININE RISING:
WOMEN IN THE FOOTSTEPS OF MOSHIACH"

"CONVERSATIONS FROM THE EDGE OF HUMAN POTENTIAL"
Global Geula Summit

THE FIRST TIME G-D GAVE ADAM THE GIFT OF WOMAN, IT DIDN'T GO SO WELL. HE REJECTED HER. THE MYSTICAL SOURCES SAY HER LIGHT FELL INTO DARK ENERGY, FEMININITY IN ITS FALLEN STATE BECAUSE SHE WAS UNABLE TO GIVE HER GIFTS. THE LOWEST LEVEL OF FEMININITY IS DESPAIR, REJECTION, UNHOLINESS.

The dark side of femininity needs to be disarmed, dissolved, healed.

JEALOUSY, ANGER, VENGEFUL, DEJECTED, REJECTED ☹ WHENEVER WE EXPERIENCE THE DARK, FALLEN STATE OF FEMININITY (THAT WE DON'T WANT TO ADMIT LURKS IN US, TOO), WE REALIZE THERE'S A SPARK OF GOOD IN IT. SHE WANTED TO GIVE, HE COULDN'T RECEIVE WHAT SHE HAD TO GIVE.

We open to the feminine nature, above the masculine.

WHEN WE RISE ABOVE TO THIS HIGHER LEVEL, IF OUR GIFTS ARE REJECTED, WE DON'T TAKE IT PERSONALLY.

IT'S WHEN WE THINK WE ARE EQUAL, AND OUR GIFTS ARE REJECTED, THAT WE FEEL THE PAIN OF REJECTION.

SOUL ADVENTURE #52

Where might you be in exile in your life?
How can you adjust the crown of your soul in your daily life?

The higher feminine is the crown.

WE HAVE TO UNDERSTAND WHAT IT MEANS TO WEAR A CROWN.

She is the Crown of Creation.

- ◆ PRESENCE ◆ BEINGNESS ◆
- ◆ RECEIVING FROM THE DIVINE SO THAT WE HAVE WHAT TO GIVE
- ◆ EGOLESS – IT'S NOT ABOUT WHO IS RIGHT, IT'S ABOUT HAVING A BIGGER VISION
- ◆ SUFFICIENT ◆ COMPASSIONATE
- ◆ LOVING ◆ SOFT

Coming out of exile to ourself & into the crown, into Malchut & royalty.

Holy Sparks
WWW.HOLYSPARKS.COM
©2020 Rae Shagalov

REBBETZIN TAMAR TABACK
SHIFRA CHANA HENDRIE
"FEMININE RISING:
WOMEN IN THE FOOTSTEPS OF MOSHIACH"

The ultimate goal is for Hashem and His Name to be One.

EMBRACING EACH OTHER AS LEGITIMATE EXPRESSIONS OF G-D'S LIGHT.

Shema LISTEN — PATIENCE & TRUST THAT THIS IS EMERGING IN ITS OWN TIME, IN ITS OWN WAY.

Yisrael — SPEAK IT TO YOUR HEART, STRAIGHT TO G-D.

MAKE G-D THE CENTER OF YOUR UNIVERSE. TAKE YOURSELF OUT OF THE CENTER AND PUT G-D THERE.

Hashem UNCOMPREHENSIBLE ETERNITY — G-D'S UNREVEALED ONENESS, STILL IN DARKNESS. HEALING THE WORLD THROUGH OUR FAITH AND CONSCIOUS CHOICES. BRINGING THE ONENESS OF G-D INTO OUR CONSCIOUSNESS,

E-lokeinu — OUR G-D RELATING TO US IN THE MOMENT.

Hashem OUR MASTER — WE STRIVE TO CONNECT TO G-D'S FULL, TRANSCENDENT BEING.

Echod THERE IS ONLY ONE POWER IN THE WORLD. WE EACH HAVE OUR PIECE AND WE MAKE SPACE FOR EVERYONE ELSE'S PIECE. TOGETHER, WE REVEAL G-D'S LIGHT INTO THE WORLD.

"CONVERSATIONS FROM THE EDGE OF HUMAN POTENTIAL"
Global Geula Summit

SOUL ADVENTURE #53

What has G-d sent you as a blessing?
Write 25 things you are grateful for.

Darkness contains a light that is so sublime that it cannot be experienced directly.

WE EARN IT THROUGH THE WORK WE DO IN TRANSFORMING THE DARKNESS TO LIGHT.

Gratitude helps us see G‑d's good in everything.

ב"ה

GRATITUDE BRINGS MORE JOY AND PEACE INTO YOUR LIFE AND INTO THE WORLD.

THE SOURCE OF ALL OF OUR BLESSINGS.

Gratitude helps us practice now what it will be like in Geulah when we will only see good. Gratitude channels Geulah into our life.

STOP. RIGHT NOW, PAUSE AND THANK G‑D FOR 3 THINGS.

Gratitude is a tool we can use in any moment to co-create Geulah with G‑d.

THIS IS ONE WAY YOU CAN BRING MORE G‑DLINESS INTO THE WORLD.

G‑d is designing your life for YOU!

THERE IS NOTHING RANDOM IN THE UNIVERSE.

This is the last generation of galus (exile) and the first generation of geulah (redemption).

GRATITUDE UNITES THE TWO.

GRATITUDE TRAINS US TO BE AWARE OF THE LEVEL OF WORLD WHERE GEULAH EXISTS BUT HAS NOT YET BEEN FULLY REVEALED.

What has G‑d sent you as a blessing?

AT YOUR SHABBOS TABLE, HAVE EACH PERSON SHARE SOMETHING FROM THE WEEK FOR WHICH YOU ARE GRATEFUL TO HASHEM.

WE CAN SEE! WE CAN HEAR! WE CAN EAT! WE CAN WALK! WE CAN BREATHE!

SAY TO YOUR FRIENDS, "TELL ME SOMETHING YOU'RE GRATEFUL FOR TODAY."

Publicize the miracles and blessings of your life.

DR. RIVKAH LAMBERT ADLER
SHIFRA CHANA HENDRIE
"GRATITUDE, GEULA & HEALING YOUR HEART"

"CONVERSATIONS FROM THE EDGE OF HUMAN POTENTIAL"
Global Geula Summit

Holy Sparks

SOUL ADVENTURE #54

Write 10 things you appreciate about the people in your life.

Pleasure is the innermost point of connection with G-d.

ב"ה

כֶּתֶר

Crown
Corona

WHEN YOU FOCUS ON THE GOOD IN YOUR LIFE, G-D WILL SURELY SEND YOU MORE!

THE CORE EXPERIENCE OF THE SOUL IS PLEASURE AND DELIGHT WITH G-D. GRATITUDE CONNECTS US TO THIS PLEASURE AND DELIGHT THROUGH APPRECIATING ALL OF THE BLESSINGS, LARGE AND SMALL THAT G-D GIVES US.

GRATITUDE IS THE GOAL AND PURPOSE OF THIS WORLD.

NOW, AND IN THE DAYS OF MOSHIACH.

Gratitude puts you in the moment in your most expansive soul to delight in what is.

Gratitude helps us deepen our connection to G-d. APPRECIATING THE GOOD INCREASES OUR AWE AND WONDER AT HOW MANY BLESSINGS G-D IS SPRINKLING ON US IN ANY GIVEN MOMENT.

Everything we experience is meant to bring us closer to G-d.

G-D PERFORMS KINDNESS FOR US ALL DAY LONG, BUT WE DON'T USUALLY NOTICE IT. GRATITUDE HELPS US SEE IT.

Everything G-d does is ultimately for our benefit.

IN GEULAH, EVERYTHING WILL BE REVEALED GOOD.

We each have each other in a way that we need, in a way that enhances us.

REMEMBER TO APPRECIATE THE PEOPLE IN YOUR LIFE.

Notice the good in your life and in the world. This is how to find G-d.

DR. RIVKAH LAMBERT ADLER
SHIFRA CHANA HENDRIE
"GRATITUDE, GEULA & HEALING YOUR HEART"

"CONVERSATIONS FROM THE EDGE OF HUMAN POTENTIAL"

Global Geula Summit

Holy Sparks
WWW.HOLYSPARKS.COM
©2020 Rae Shagalov

בס״ד

SOUL ADVENTURE #55

How could you nurture the Divine Spark within you?
How can you make the world purer, brighter & holier today?

It's not what I want, but what does life want from me?

The only way to truly be free is to commit to making the world purer, brighter, and holier.

What we feel needs to inspire us to pray.

THE THING WE ARE TRYING TO FREE OURSELF FROM IS ACTUALLY WHAT GIVES US OUR PURPOSE. G-D CREATED US FROM THIS WORLD SO THAT WE WILL ELEVATE IT. THE WORLD HAS TO BE ELEVATED FROM THE BOTTOM, FROM THE LOWEST PART OF OUR EXPERIENCE.

בס"ד

We are here to serve our Creator. This is how to be joyous and free.

Your Soul is part of the Creator, NOT part of the creation.

There is a Divine Spark inside of you!

LIVING ACCORDING TO G-D'S LAW IS THE ULTIMATE FREEDOM.

THE SOUL WITHOUT THE BODY CANNOT ACHIEVE ITS PURPOSE.

NURTURE IT.

Breath is G-d telling us we matter.

The Holy Sparks are calling us to elevate them.

SHIMONA TZUKERNIK
SHIFRA CHANA HENDRIE
"FREE YOURSELF TO BE YOURSELF: LIVING THE LIFE YOU'RE BEING CALLED TO"
"CONVERSATIONS FROM THE EDGE OF HUMAN POTENTIAL"
Global Geula Summit

Holy Sparks

WWW.HOLYSPARKS.COM
©2020 Rae Shagalov

SOUL ADVENTURE #56

Just be present to who you are.

ב"ה

Just be present to who you are.

Our darkness, our struggles, and failures, and limitations are also part of G-d's own purpose.

WHEN YOU SEE THAT YOUR STRUGGLES ARE YOUR PURPOSE, THEN YOU FREE YOURSELF TO BE YOURSELF TO LIVE THE LIFE YOU'RE BEING CALLED TO.

G-d wants us to make ourselves into a sanctuary so that He can dwell within us.

IF YOU WANT TO BE WHO YOU TRULY ARE, YOU HAVE TO BE WILLING TO EMBRACE YOUR EARTHINESS, THE DUALITY OF BODY AND SOUL.

YOU HAVE TO HOLD THE SPACE FOR YOUR FEELINGS AND LIMITATIONS WITH COMPASSION.

To feel heard and seen is one of the greatest gifts you can give to another.

You can deal with shadow feelings by flooding them with light!

BUT WE ALSO NEED TO DO A CHESHBON HANEFESH, AN ACCOUNTING OF THE SOUL, WITH COMPASSION. THERE IS AN ANIMAL SOUL THAT DRIVES YOU AND ALL OF THE WOUNDED PARTS THAT ARE PART OF YOUR HERO'S JOURNEY.

The fortitude of your spirit is breathtaking!

SHIMONA TZUKERNIK
SHIFRA CHANA HENDRIE
"FREE YOURSELF TO BE YOURSELF:
LIVING THE LIFE YOU'RE BEING CALLED TO"
"CONVERSATIONS FROM THE EDGE OF HUMAN POTENTIAL"
Global Geula Summit

Holy Sparks

SOUL ADVENTURE #57

Where are you?

WHY ARE YOU HERE RIGHT NOW? WHAT ARE YOU LONGING FOR? WHAT DO YOU NEED THAT WOULD SUPPORT YOU? WHAT DO YOU WANT FOR THE WORLD?

בס"ד

Holy Sparks

we are all little pieces of the Divine puzzle.

LIKE A GIANT JIGSAW PUZZLE SPREAD ACROSS THE UNIVERSE, WE TURN OURSELVES OVER AND LOOK AT OUR OWN PIECE OF THE PUZZLE. WE LOOK FOR THE NEXT PIECE THAT IS SIMILAR TO US AND FORM A COMMUNITY. THEN WE LOOK AT THE PICTURE ON THE TOP OF THE PUZZLE SO WE UNDERSTAND WHERE WE'RE GOING, AND HOW WE UNIQUELY FIT IN. WITHOUT OUR UNIQUE PIECE, THE PUZZLE WOULD BE INCOMPLETE.

Where are you?

WHY ARE YOU HERE RIGHT NOW? WHAT ARE YOU LONGING FOR? WHAT DO YOU NEED THAT WOULD SUPPORT YOU? WHAT DO YOU WANT FOR THE WORLD?

Turn your challenges into miraculous Divine power!

Shine your light!

when you shine your unique light and truth of your soul, it illuminates all of us.

Allow something NEW to come into this world.

Living Geulah

is connecting to the Light of G·d in the future world. This new light is shining stronger and stronger, brighter and brighter!

YOU ARE ON A DIVINE MISSION!

SHIFRA CHANA HENDRIE "LIVING PURPOSE: WHAT'S POSSIBLE NOW

Global Geula Summit

Holy Sparks

בס״ד

SOUL ADVENTURE #58

Go to www.Chabad.org
and learn some Chassidus.
Record some ideas from
what you learned below.

בס"ד

If you really want to tap into the Light of the future, if you really want to see the world the way G‑d sees it, you need to tap into the light of Chassidus, the mystical Torah.

Torah is the Blueprint for Creation.

WHEN YOU CONNECT TO THAT BLUEPRINT, YOU GET TO COCREATE WHAT COMES INTO THE WORLD.

No piece of darkness can be left unelevated..

WE HAVE TO CONNECT TO THE ESSENCE OF G‑D'S WISDOM IN ORDER TO BRING OUT THE ESSENCE OF OUR OWN POWER.

The impossible is completely possible to G‑d.

Ask. Allow. Receive.

The darkness and the challenge, the obstacle contains within it the access to your soul's miraculous powers.

G‑D IS CREATING THE HEAVEN AND EARTH CONTINUOUSLY, RECREATING THE WORLD IN EVERY INSTANT WITH NEW LIGHT AND NEW POSSIBILITIES.

Use every bit of your nature to serve G‑d.

You are in the special forces and you are here to serve.

WE ARE WEAVING TOGETHER HEAVEN AND EARTH.

SHIFRA CHANA HENDRIE
"LIVING PURPOSE: WHAT'S POSSIBLE NOW"

Holy Sparks

WWW.HOLYSPARKS.COM
©2020 Rae Shagalov

Global Geula Summit
"CONVERSATIONS FROM THE EDGE OF HUMAN POTENTIAL"

Notes

The darkness is a portal to your soul.

GEULAH IS EACH OF US SHINING OUR UNIQUE LIGHT FOR EVERYONE, AND EVERYONE RECOGNIZING AND APPRECIATING EACH OTHER'S LIGHT, AND WE'RE ALTOGETHER PART OF SOMETHING BIGGER. THIS IS RECTIFIED HUMANITY.

Be humble and open. Turn the past into wisdom and growth, and open to a new future.

CONNECT TO THE LIGHT OF THE FUTURE.

Humility helps you become a clear channel for pure G☀dliness, a vessel for Divine Light.

We're all moving from finite to infinite◆

DON'T LOOK BACK. LOOK FORWARD.

Ask. Align. Allow.

PRAY @ WORK ON YOURSELF

Let's see how high we can go until the whole world's lifted up!

Each of us is a channel for Redemption

in our own personal universe◆

WHEN YOU TAKE YOUR PLACE IN THE COSMIC UNFOLDING TO BE A PARTNER WITH G-D IN THE PROCESS OF REDEMPTION, YOU'RE CONNECTING TO DIFFERENT LAWS OF NATURE, YOU TAP INTO THE REALM OF MIRACLES.

Holy Sparks

Global Geula Summit

SHIFRA CHANA HENDRIE "LIVING PURPOSE: WHAT'S POSSIBLE NOW"

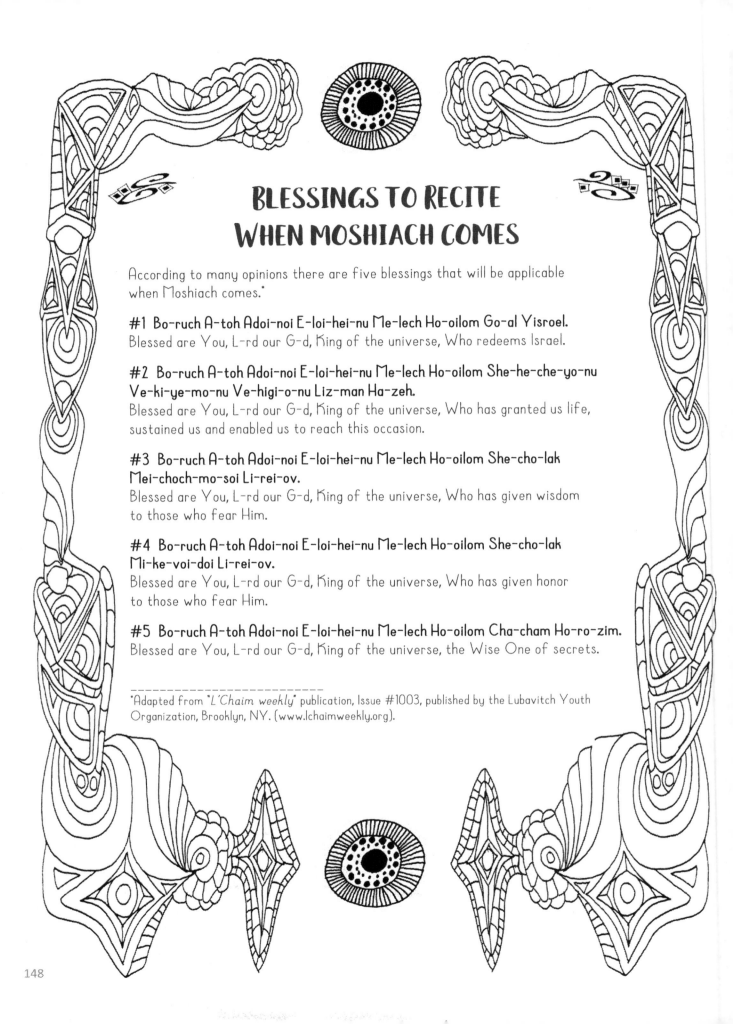

BLESSINGS TO RECITE
WHEN MOSHIACH COMES

According to many opinions there are five blessings that will be applicable when Moshiach comes.*

#1 Bo-ruch A-toh Adoi-noi E-loi-hei-nu Me-lech Ho-oilom Go-al Yisroel.
Blessed are You, L-rd our G-d, King of the universe, Who redeems Israel.

#2 Bo-ruch A-toh Adoi-noi E-loi-hei-nu Me-lech Ho-oilom She-he-che-yo-nu Ve-ki-ye-mo-nu Ve-higi-o-nu Liz-man Ha-zeh.
Blessed are You, L-rd our G-d, King of the universe, Who has granted us life, sustained us and enabled us to reach this occasion.

#3 Bo-ruch A-toh Adoi-noi E-loi-hei-nu Me-lech Ho-oilom She-cho-lak Mei-choch-mo-soi Li-rei-ov.
Blessed are You, L-rd our G-d, King of the universe, Who has given wisdom to those who fear Him.

#4 Bo-ruch A-toh Adoi-noi E-loi-hei-nu Me-lech Ho-oilom She-cho-lak Mi-ke-voi-doi Li-rei-ov.
Blessed are You, L-rd our G-d, King of the universe, Who has given honor to those who fear Him.

#5 Bo-ruch A-toh Adoi-noi E-loi-hei-nu Me-lech Ho-oilom Cha-cham Ho-ro-zim.
Blessed are You, L-rd our G-d, King of the universe, the Wise One of secrets.

_____

*Adapted from "L'Chaim weekly" publication, Issue #1003, published by the Lubavitch Youth Organization, Brooklyn, NY. (www.lchaimweekly.org).

List of Things to Do
to Get Ready for Moshiach

בס"ד

❧ GLOSSARY ❧

Adam HaRishon:	The first man
Ahavas Yisrael:	Love for a fellow Jew
Aish:	Fire
Amalek:	An enemy of the Jews, recurring throughout the generations; the embodiment of evil and doubt
Avodah:	Prayer; service to G-d
Bashert:	Meant to be; sent from G-d
Bais/Beis Hamikdash:	The Holy Temple
Ben:	Son
Bina:	Understanding
Bris:	Covenant
Chochma:	Wisdom
Chassid/Chassidic:	Chassidic life and philosophy is a branch of Orthodox Judaism founded in 18th-century Eastern Europe by Rabbi Israel Baal Shem Tov, based on spiritual reawakening through Torah, mysticism and Ahavas Yisrael.
Chassidus:	Collection of Chassidic teachings primarily as taught by the Chabad Rebbes
Cheshbon HaNefesh:	Introspection; literally, "Accounting of the Soul"
Chesed:	The quality of lovingkindness
Choson/Chossan:	Bridegroom
Daas/Daat:	Knowledge
Daven/Davening:	Pray/Praying
Devekut:	Cleaving to G-d
Eliahu Hanavi:	Elijah, the Prophet
Emunah:	Faith
Ezer Kenegdo:	Helpmate
Geula/Geulah:	The Time of Redemption when the world will be filled with the knowledge of G-d
Gemarah:	The collection of Rabbinic writings constituting the basis of religious authority in Torah law
Gevurah:	The quality of severity, limitation
Golus:	Exile from G-dliness

Hakodesh Baruch Hu:	The Blessed Holy One
Hashem:	G-d; literally, "The Name"
Hitbodedut:	Self-isolation or seclusion; the Jewish meditation practice of speaking privately with G-d
Kabbalah:	"Tradition," the general term for Jewish mysticism; authentic Jewish mysticism is an integral part of Torah
Kavanah:	Intention, concentration
Kavod:	Honor and respect
Kishkes:	Literally means intestines or guts as in a "gut feeling"
Klal Yisrael:	The collective body of the Jewish people
Klippah:	An evil shell (so to speak) that obstructs holiness
Kodesh, Kedushah:	Holy or holiness; to separate and sanctify what is G-dly from what comes from the opposite of G-dliness or holiness
Kohen:	A member of the priestly tribe of the Jewish people
Kohen Gadol:	The High Priest who served in the Holy Temple in Jerusalem
Kvetch:	To complain
Lashon Hara:	Gossip, evil speech
Malach:	An angel
Malchus:	The quality of royalty
Mishega'ass:	Foolishness
Mishkan:	Tabernacle
Moshiach:	The Anointed Redeemer, Messiah
Mitzvahs or Mitzvot:	Divine commandments (that connect us to G-d)
Moshe Rabbeinu:	Moses, our teacher
N'aseh v'Nishmah:	To do and to hear; The Jewish people accepted the mitzvahs at Mt. Sinai unconditionally
Parnassah:	Livelihood
Pinchas:	Grandson of Aaron, and son of Elazar, the High Priest
Ra:	Evil
Rabbeinu:	Our teacher
Ribono Shel Olam:	Master of the Universe
Ruach:	Spirit; one of the levels of the soul

Satan:	The angel created to serve G-d in the role of provocateur
Shabbos/Shabbat:	The Sabbath day of rest
Shalom:	Peace
Shalom Bayis:	A peaceful home
Shechina:	The Divine Presence as it manifests in this world
Shekel:	A coin of Israel
Simcha:	Happiness, joy
Shlemazel:	An unlucky, hapless person
Shmooze:	To chat
Teferes/Teferet	The soul's quality of beauty, harmony, balance
Tefillah:	Prayer
Tehillim/Psalms:	The book of 150 songs and praises of G-d by King David
Teshuva:	Repentance; returning to the righteous path of Torah and G-d
Tikkun:	Repair, rectification; our world is considered the world of Tikkun
Tohu:	The world of chaos that preceded this world, according to Kabbalah
Torah:	The Five Books of Moses; the entire body of Jewish knowledge; G-d's thought and will condensed in a physical scroll
Tumah:	Impurity
Tzaddik/Tzadekes:	A pious, saintly man/woman
Tzedakah:	Charity
Tzimtzum:	In Jewish mysticism, the process whereby G-d concealed Himself in order to create this world with free choice
Tzitzit/Tzitzis	A fringed, 4-cornered undergarment worn to fulfill a mitzvah
Yartzeit:	Anniversary of a person's death
Yehuda:	One of the sons of our patriarch and matriarch, Jacob and Leah
Yetzer Hara:	The inclination to do wrong
Yetzer Tov:	The inclination to do what is good and right
Zohar:	A commentary on the Torah which is a central mystical work of Jewish mysticism

❧ A NOTE ABOUT G-D* ❧

WHY SHOULD YOU TALK TO HASHEM?**

There are many benefits to talking to G-d. You will feel calmer and happier when you know that you are never truly alone. You will increase your faith, improve your character, and have more energy to meet your challenges when you are connected to G-d's infinite source of strength. Hitbodedut (meditation) cleanses your soul, connects you to holiness, and improves all of your relationships with G-d, other people, and even with yourself.

For best results and a deeper relationship, make an appointment with Hashem every day. Dedicate a set amount of time each day, and don't let anything stop you! Start with just one minute, if you have to, and just show up — even if you don't feel like it or you have nothing to say. By the end of 30 days, you will wonder how you ever lived without talking to G-d every day.

WHY IS G-D REFERRED TO AS "HE"?

Isn't G-d infinitely beyond any gender? Yes, G-d is beyond gender, but we're not. Through the Torah, Chassidut, and the mystical Kabbalah, we learn the secrets of how G-d created the universe. When the kabbalists describe the exquisite dance and love relationship between the transcendental and the imminent presence of G-d in this world, the transcendent aspect of the infinite Holy One is presented in the masculine. The immanent divine presence or Shechinah and we, who reach for the relationship, are described in the feminine.

---

*To protect G-d's name, we don't spell it out completely. The Jewish people do not write G-d's name in a place where it may be discarded, erased, or carried into an unclean place. Please note that this book should not be taken into a bathroom.

**We often use the Hebrew word "Hashem," which means "The Name," instead of using G-d's name. Treating G-d's name with this extra reverence is a way to protect the holiness and sanctity of G-d's name.

To learn more about Jewish meditation and get inspired to start a daily practice, you may order Rae Shagalov's beautifully illustrated book, "The Secret Art of Talking to G-d," on Amazon at: http://bit.ly/talking-to-G-d

❧INTRODUCTION TO THE JOYFULLY JEWISH SERIES ❧

I love being Jewish! But I didn't always. In fact, I left Judaism for 10 years and became a "spiritual tourist." You see, when I was growing up, I never learned about the spiritual secrets of authentic Torah. I thought there was no such thing as Jewish meditation or Jewish spirituality. I didn't even think Jews were supposed to be happy!

Then, through developing my craft as a calligrapher, I discovered the mystical secrets of Judaism. When I began to explore the alef bet, letter-by-letter, the holy Hebrew letters led me on a quest to discover a deep, soulful, joyful Judaism I never knew existed.

By the grace of G-d, from the very beginning of my Torah learning I discovered my talent as a Jewish artist. I realized that what I was learning was so profound, I wanted to be sure to review my notes over and over again and to share these Torah secrets with others. I began to write my notes in calligraphy. I had classical training and was already a professional calligrapher, and I began to "doodle". I knew that people would enjoy coloring in my doodles as they read and absorbed the Jewish wisdom on each page.

I love to learn the secrets of Torah, about the intricacies of our soul, and how the universe is designed to help us transform this world into a dwelling place for G-d. With the help of G-d, over the last 30 years, I've gone to thousands of classes and written more than 3,000 pages of calligraphy Artnotes that capture the essence of each class. This Jewish wisdom from hundreds of our greatest Torah leaders gives us a very important message for our special time at the threshold of the Messianic Era* of peace. I call these Artnotes the "field notes of the last generation of exile and the first generation of Geula.** They are being published as a complete collection in a series called, *Gevaltig!*

If you would like to help support the publication of this important wisdom or dedicate a book in honor or memory of a loved one, please contact me at: INFO@HOLYSPARKS.COM

---

*Moshiach & the Messianic Era: Moshiach is the Jewish messiah, the long-awaited Redeemer who will bring us out of the exile of this world into an amazing world filled with the revelation of G-dliness in every aspect of Creation. The word Moshiach in Hebrew means "anointed". One of the principles of Jewish faith according to Maimonides is that one day there will arise a dynamic Jewish leader, a direct descendant of the Davidic dynasty, who will rebuild the Temple in Jerusalem and gather Jews from all over the world and bring them back to the Land of Israel. In every generation, Moshiach is ready to be revealed when we have finished preparing the world to receive him. Every man, woman and child has an individual responsibility and priviledge to work to bring about Moshiach's coming, using his or her unique talents and situation.

**The Lubavitcher Rebbe, Rabbi Menachem Mendel Schneerson, taught us that we must -- NOW -- "live with the Redemption," experience a foretaste of it and anticipate it in our daily conduct. This means living our lives in a way that parallels the way we would live in the time of the Redemption.

The Joyfully Jewish series began with the Joyfully Jewish Family and Adult Coloring Book that integrates the relaxing, meditative art of coloring with deep Chassidic secrets of Judaism. It includes fun designs to color, unique Jewish quotes from contemporary Jewish masters written in beautiful calligraphy, and is an uplifting introduction to Jewish spirituality. The graphic images from that coloring book came from my Artnotes sketchbooks.

The Joyfully Jewish series of Artnotes includes many full-page and smaller images to color, but unlike the coloring book, it is much richer and fuller in calligraphy text and field notes from the Jewish wisdom classes in which they were drawn. Most of the pages are copies of the original Artnotes pages, just as I wrote and drew them during the classes.

The first volume of the series is "Create Your Joyfully Jewish Life!" (available on Amazon.com). It's a six week creative journaling workbook, filled with calligraphy Artnotes, Soul Adventures, & coloring pages to guide you, step-by-step, to create a happy, healthy, and meaningul Jewish life. It's a good place to start to organize and energize your Jewish Journey.

My goal for the Joyfully Jewish series is to provide you with a pleasant, fun, and interactive, journey into Jewish learning. It's very important for you to engage with what you're learning so that you can really integrate it into your life in a joyful way. There are many areas for you to color and blank pages for you to record your thoughts, insights, good resolutions, doodles and dreams for your life and the Messianic Era soon to come, please G-d.

Some of the Soul Adventures in this book were developed in Joyfully Jewish workshops that I have led. If you are interested in a workshop for your organization or birthday, in person or via Zoom, contact me at the email address below.

I would love to see your colorful creations, so let's connect! Feel free to email me with questions, suggestions, personal insights, or reflections you'd like to share – and, of course, pictures of your coloring. Please share them with me via email at: INFO@HOLYSPARKS.COM or on any of my social media channels listed at the front of this book.

It is with great humility that I offer to you this volume of Artnotes in my Joyfully Jewish series. It is my great hope that they will inspire you, deepen your love of Torah, increase your motivation to do mitzvahs, and help you feel closer to G-d in every moment of your life.

May G-d keep you from all manner of harm and distress and bless the works of your hands with success, in good health, with great joy and abundant livelihood, and may you always be Joyfully Jewish!

May you be blessed with success and only good things!

Rae Shagalov

Holy Sparks

❧10 WAYS TO BE JOYFULLY JEWISH❧

The most important principle in the Torah is the protection of Jewish life. It's more important than Shabbat, more important than holidays or even fasting on Yom Kippur. Right now, in Israel and everywhere, Jews must stand together in unity and do whatever possible to protect Jewish life.

The Lubavitcher Rebbe, Rabbi Menachem M. Schneerson, teaches that there are ten important Mitzvahs* we can do to protect life. We urgently need your help to increase in mitzvahs and merits for the Jewish people. Please choose a mitzvah to begin or improve:

1) AHAVAS YISROEL: Behave with love towards another Jew.
2) LEARN TORAH: Join a Torah class.
3) Make sure that Jewish children get a TORAH-TRUE EDUCATION.
4) Affix kosher MEZUZAS on all doorways of the house.
5) For men and boys over 13: Put on TEFILLIN every weekday.
6) Give CHARITY.
7) Buy JEWISH HOLY BOOKS and study them.
8) LIGHT SHABBAT & YOM TOV CANDLES, a Mitzvah for women and girls.
9) Eat and drink only KOSHER FOOD.
10) Observe the laws of JEWISH FAMILY PURITY.

In addition, the Rebbe urges that:

Every Jewish man, woman and child should have a letter written for them in a Sefer Torah.**

Every person should study either the Rambam's Yad Hachazakah –Code of Jewish Law – or the Rambam's Sefer HaMitzvos.

Concerning Moshiach, the Rebbe stated, "The time for our redemption has arrived!" Everyone should prepare themselves for Moshiach's coming by increasing acts of goodness and kindness and by studying about what the future redemption will be like. May we merit to see the fulfillment of the Rebbe's prophecy, NOW!

----

*Mitzvahs are Divine Commandments that connect us to G-d.

**There are several Torah scrolls being written to unite Jewish people and protect Jewish life. Letters for children can be purchased for only $1 via the Internet at: http://www.kidstorah.org

For more information about how to be Joyfully Jewish, visit:

Holysparks.com	Moshiach.net	Chabad.org
Jewishwoman.org	Jewishkids.org	Maayon.com
Meaningfullife.com	Inner.org	Torahcafe.com

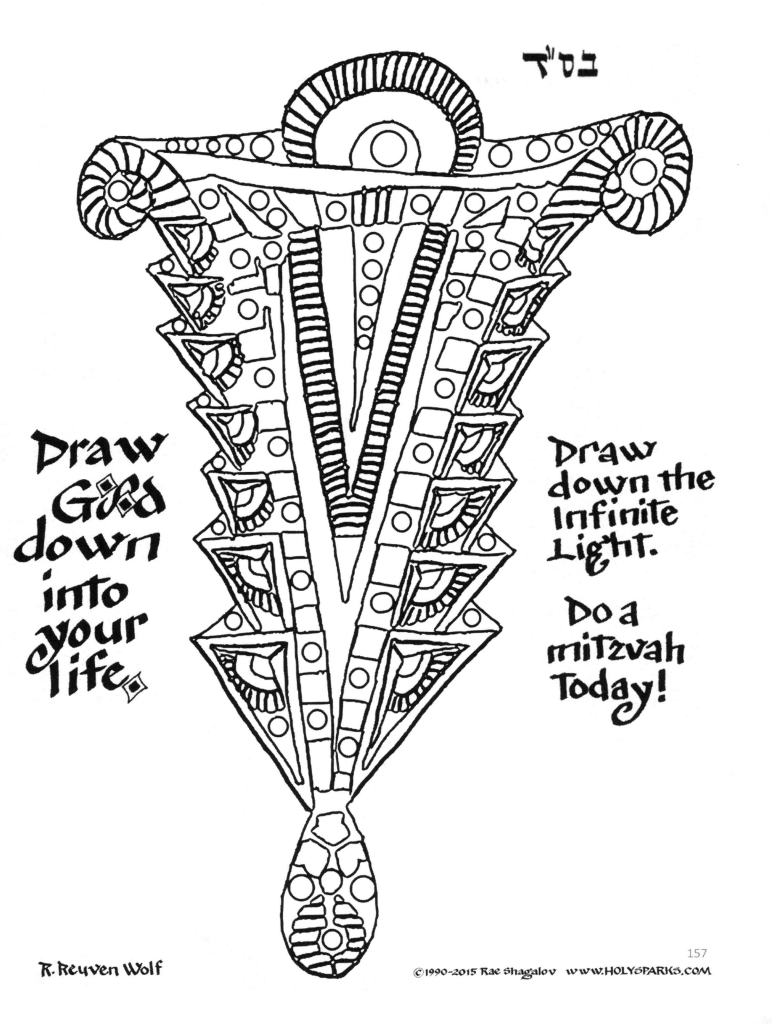

בס"ד

Draw
G-d
down
into
your
life.

Draw
down the
Infinite
Light.

Do a
mitzvah
Today!

R. Reuven Wolf

157

©1990-2015 Rae Shagalov www.HOLYSPARKS.COM

৯ 7 SPECIAL MITZVAHS FOR RIGHTEOUS GENTILES ৯

"The word 'commandment' is a translation of the Hebrew word mitzvah, which also means 'connection.' By observing G-d's commandments, a person becomes connected with G-d's infinite will and wisdom and thereby elicits a G-dly light which shines onto his or her soul.
-Likutei Torah, Rabbi Shneur Zalman of Liadi-

"The non-Jews have the full length and breadth of Torah—they just have a different role in it. The role of every person is to be a good person, to bring divine light, to draw down G-dliness into the world. To do it as a Jew, as a non-Jew, it doesn't matter. It's the same light, the same Godly energy."

-Rabbi Yakov Cohen-

There are seven special mitzvahs, known as the Seven Laws of Noah, which are the minimal Torah observance for non-Jews. The Noahide commandments are those that G-d gave to Adam and his descendants and, after the flood, to Noah and his descendants. They are binding upon all of humanity, and were included in the Torah when G-d gave it to the People of Israel at Mount Sinai. Men and women are equal in their responsibility to observe the Seven Universal Laws.

By learning the Torah laws that pertain to all people and performing these mitzvahs (commandments or Torah laws), the righteous people of all nations help perfect this world to a new state of universal holiness, wisdom and peace. "The Seven Noahide Laws" are a sacred inheritance of all the Children of Noah (non-Jews or gentiles), one that every person can use to have a fulfilling spiritual life.

Besides the Seven Universal Laws, the Children of Noah have traditionally taken it upon themselves to fulfill the commandments of honoring mother and father, giving charity, and studying Torah. When a Gentile resolves to fulfill the Seven Universal Laws, his or her soul is elevated. This person becomes one of the "Chasidei Umot Haolam" (Pious Ones of the Nations) and receives a share of the World to Come.

To find out more about the Seven Noahide Laws, go to:
www.asknoah.org
www.noahide.org

❧THE SEVEN NOAHIDE LAWS ❧

Believe in One G-d (Prohibition of Idolatry)

Acknowledge that there is only one G-d who is Infinite and Supreme above all things. Do not replace that Supreme Being with finite idols or other gods. This mitzvah includes such acts as prayer, study and meditation.

Keep the Name of G-d Holy (Prohibition of Blasphemy)

Respect the Creator. As frustrated and angry as you may be, don't blame it on G-d, Who loves you so much He created you and breathes life into you every moment.

Respect Human Life (Prohibition of Murder)

Human life is holy, as man was created in the image of G-d. Every person is of irreplaceable value. Every human being is an entire world; to save a life is to save that entire world. To destroy a life is to destroy an entire world.

Respect the Rights and Property of Others (Prohibition of Theft)

Be honest in all your business dealings. Express your trust in G-d as the Provider of life and your livelihood.

Respect the Family (Prohibition of Illicit Relations)

Respect the institution of marriage. Marriage is a most Divine act. The marriage of a man and a woman is a reflection of the oneness of G-d and His creation. Disloyalty in marriage and other forms of forbidden relationships destroy that oneness.

Respect All Life (Prohibition of Eating Meat from a Live Animal)

Respect G-d's creatures. At first, Man was forbidden to consume meat. After the Great Flood, he was permitted - but with a warning: Do not cause unnecessary suffering to any creature.

Establish Courts of Justice

Justice is G-d's business, but we are given the charge to lay down necessary laws and enforce them whenever we can. When we right the wrongs of society, we are acting as partners in creating the perfection of the world.

‿ ABOUT HOLY SPARKS ‿

Holy Sparks is dedicated to spreading the light of authentic Jewish spirituality and wisdom. Holy Sparks provides and promotes Jewish knowledge, awareness and practice as it applies to people of all faiths and nationalities, regardless of affiliation or background. Holy Sparks helps spiritual seekers, particularly the Jewish people, and others who are looking for inspiration and encouragement, to discover and fulfill their individual talents and potential for serving G-d and mankind through increasing acts of goodness, kindness, and holiness.

‿ ABOUT RAE SHAGALOV ‿

Master calligrapher Rae Shagalov is the author of the Amazon bestseller, "The Secret Art of Talking to G-d" and the "Joyfully Jewish" series of interactive calligraphy and coloring books for adults and families. Rae is eager to share the beauty and wisdom of Torah through her 3,000 pages of beautifully designed Artnotes that reveal the special message of this exciting time in Jewish History. Rae has combined her experience as a creativity coach, her talent as a Jewish artist, and her fascinating spiritual search for the true meaning of life to produce these beautiful Jewish Artnotes. Rae's books provide her readers with very practical, joy-based action steps for infusing authentic Jewish spirituality into their daily lives. Rae offers Creative Clarity Coaching for women who want to use their creativity, discover their Life Purpose and elevate their spiritual growth. She is also an innovative educator who develops the talents of children at Emek Hebrew Academy in Los Angeles. Find out more about Rae Shagalov's coaching & workshops at: www.holysparks.com.

‿ CONNECT WITH RAE ‿

Sign up to receive free art, coloring pages
and Rae's Soul Tips newsletter!
Go to: www.holysparks.com

LET'S CONNECT!

Facebook.com/soultips
Pinterest.com/holysparks
Twitter.com/holysparks
Youtube.com/holysparksbooks

There's a Holy Spark in each of us
that's hidden very well;
when it's revealed, we make our world
a place where G‑d can dwell.

בָּרוּךְ אַתָּה אַדֹנָ-י אֱ-לֹהֵינוּ מֶלֶךְ הָעוֹלָם אֲשֶׁר קִדְּשָׁנוּ בְּמִצְוֹתָיו וְצִוָּנוּ לְהַדְלִיק נֵר שֶׁל שַׁבָּת קֹדֶשׁ

TRANSLITERATION:
BARUCH A-TA A-DO-NAY
ELO-HEI-NU ME-LECH HA-O-LAM
A-SHER KI-DI-SHA-NU
BI-MITZ-VO-TAV VI-TZI-VA-NOO
LI-HAD-LEEKNER SHEL SHA-BAT
KO-DESH.

TRANSLATION:
BLESSED ARE YOU, L-RD OUR G-D,
KING OF THE UNIVERSE, WHO HAS
SANCTIFIED US WITH HIS
COMMANDMENTS, AND
COMMANDED US TO KINDLE THE
LIGHT OF THE HOLY SHABBAT.

Lighting Shabbos candles brings peace, not only to the family, lighting Shabbos candles illuminates the whole world.

~ The Zohar ~

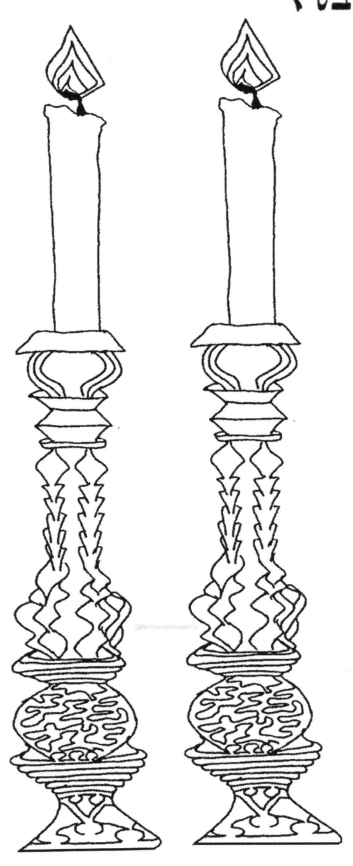

❧ WEBSITES OF THE TEACHERS ❧

Rabbi Simon Jacobson	meaningfullife.com
Rabbi Amichai Cohen	livekabbalah.com
Rabbi Asher Crispe	interinclusion.org
Rabbi Yisroel Bernath	jewishndg.com
Chaya Kaplan-Lester	chayalester.com
Rabbi Daniel Kohn	sulamyaakov.com
Rabbi David Katz	getsoulstrong.com
Rabbi Doniel Katz	elevationproject.com
Haya Baker	divineintegrationhealing.com
Rabbi Mendel Kessin	torahthinking.com
Rabbi Moshe Miller	kabbalahdecoded.com
Orit Esther Riter	dailydoseofemuna.com
Rabbi Pinchas Winston	thirtysix.org
Rabbi Aaron Raskin	bnaiavraham.org
Rivka Malka Perlman	rivkamalka.com
Rabbi Tovia Singer	outreachjudaism.org
Rabbi Avraham Arieh Trugman	thetrugmans.com
Sarah Yehudit Scneider	astillsmallvoice.org
Rabbi Reuven Wolf	maayon.com
Rabbi David Aaron	rabbidavidaaron.com
Rebbetzin Tamar Taback	thenexus.org
Dr. Rivkah Lambert Adler	tenfromthenations.com
Shimona Tzukernik	shimona.org
Shifra Chana Hendrie	gateofunity.com
Rae Shagalov	holysparks.com

❧ OTHER RESOURCES ❧

JoyfullyJewish.com	Moshiach.net	Chabad.org
Jewishwoman.org	Jewishkids.org	Maayon.com
Meaningfullife.com	Inner.org	Torahcafe.com
igrot.com/English	www.chabad.org/dailystudy	
(Write to the Rebbe)	(To learn daily Chumash/Tanya/Tehillim	

CLAIM YOUR FREE BONUS!

Sign up for your FREE bonus at:
HOLYSPARKS.COM
(Feel free to share this link with your friends!)

Will you be kind enough to do me a favor?

Please leave a review on Amazon!
Here's the link to find this and all of my other
books on Amazon:
HTTP://AMZN.TO/2AYKVET

It would be very helpful for me and those who are considering whether or not to buy Joyfully Jewish books for their own personal growth or to give as a gift to a friend if you would kindly leave a review for this book on Amazon. This will help us reach many more people with this amazing Jewish wisdom that is especially relevant to our generation to prepare the world for Moshiach. Thank you so much!

COLOPHON

The Artnotes in this book were all originally handwritten and drawn during classes. The Headings are Felix Titling and the printed text uses Catalina Clemente, Tempus Sans ITC, True Sketch & Charcuterie Flared . The Dingbats are Wingdings 2. Some of the coloring pages were digitally modified from the original Artnotes using Repper Pro.

WITH DEEP APPRECIATION & GRATITUDE TO:
Supporters: Maggie Brody & Karl Rose
My Darling Daughter & Editor: Juniper Ekman
My Dear Husband, Yosef Yitzchok Shagalov

This Publication Is Dedicated To The Rebbe,
Rabbi Menachem M. Schneerson of Lubavitch
whose teachings and inspiration lives in us, and fires us up
to try and reach heights we can't reach on our own,
to prepare the whole world for the imminent arrival of Moshiach.

IN LOVING MEMORY OF

Harav Schneur Zalman Halevi ע״ה
ben Harav Yitzchok Elchonon Halevi הי״ד Shagalov

Reb Dovid Asniel ben Reb Eliyahu ע״ה

Devora Rivka bas Reb Yosef Eliezer ע״ה

Reb Yitzchok Moshe ben Reb Dovid Asniel ע״ה

❧   May Their Souls Merit Eternal Life   ☙

AND IN HONOR OF

Mrs. Esther Shaindel bas Fraidel Chedva שתחי׳ Shagalov
and Our Dear Children and Grandchildren שיחיו
May You Always Be Joyfully Jewish!

DEDICATED BY

Rabbi & Mrs. Yosef Yitzchok and Gittel Rachel שיחיו Shagalov

To dedicate future editions in
honor or memory of your
loved ones, contact us at:
info@holysparks.com

בס"ד

This book is dedicated to
Chaya Mushka
bas Shifra Chana.
May Hashem bless her with
an immediate and miraculous
refuah shleimah!

Holy Sparks
©2020 Rae Shaqalov
WWW.HOLYSPARKS.COM

Made in the USA
San Bernardino, CA
22 July 2020